1st EDITION

Perspectives on Modern World History

The Holocaust

1st EDITION

Perspectives on Modern World History

The Holocaust

David Haugen and Susan Musser

Book Editors

GREENHAVEN PRESS
A part of Gale, Cengage Learning

GALE
CENGAGE Learning

Detroit • New York • San Francisco • New Haven, Conn • Waterville, Maine • London

Christine Nasso, *Publisher*
Elizabeth Des Chenes, *Managing Editor*

For more information, contact:
Greenhaven Press
27500 Drake Rd.
Farmington Hills, MI 48331-3535
Or you can visit our Internet site at gale.cengage.com.

For product information and technology assistance, contact us at
Gale Customer Support, 1-800-877-4253.

For permission to use material from this text or product, submit all requests online at
www.cengage.com/permissions.

Further permissions questions can be e-mailed to permissionrequest@cengage.com.

LIBRARY OF CONGRESS CATALOGING-IN-PUBLICATION DATA

The Holocaust / David Haugen and Susan Musser, book editors.
   p. cm. -- (Perspectives on modern world history)
   Includes bibliographical references and index.
ISBN 978-0-7377-5258-8 (hardcover)
1. Holocaust, Jewish (1939–1945)--Juvenile literature. I. Haugen, David M., 1969– II. Musser, Susan.
   D804.34.H643 2011
   940.53'18--dc22   2010048602

Printed in the United States of America
1 2 3 4 5 6 7 15 14 13 12 11

CONTENTS

In this article for a Czech magazine, the author asserts that Muslim Holocaust denials stem not from a factual refutation of the facts but rather from a desire to find a sore spot that will invoke Western rage.

CHAPTER 3   Personal Narratives

An American who served in the army during World War II describes the extreme emotional response he had upon seeing liberated concentration camp prisoners encountered by his unit while chasing the fleeing Nazi army into Austria.

FOREWORD

*"History cannot give us a program for the future,
but it can give us a fuller understanding of ourselves, and of our common humanity, so that we
can better face the future."*

—Robert Penn Warren,
American poet and novelist

The history of each nation is punctuated by mo-
mentous events that represent turning points for
that nation, with an impact felt far beyond its borders. These events—displaying the full range of human
capabilities, from violence, greed, and ignorance to heroism, courage, and strength—are nearly always complicated and multifaceted. Any student of history faces the
challenge of grasping the many strands that constitute
such world-changing events as wars, social movements,
and environmental disasters. But understanding these
significant historic events can be enhanced by exposure
to a variety of perspectives, whether of people involved
intimately or of ones observing from a distance of miles
or years. Understanding can also be increased by learning about the controversies surrounding such events and
exploring hot-button issues from multiple angles. Finally,
true understanding of important historic events involves
knowledge of the events' human impact—of the ways
such events affected people in their everyday lives—all
over the world.

Perspectives on Modern World History examines
global historic events from the twentieth-century onward by presenting analysis and observation from nu-
merous vantage points. Each volume offers high school,
early college level, and general interest readers a the-

matically arranged anthology of previously published materials that address a major historical event, with an emphasis on international coverage. Each volume opens with background information on the event, then presents the controversies surrounding that event, and concludes with first-person narratives from people who lived through the event or were affected by it. By providing primary sources from the time of the event, as well as relevant commentary surrounding the event, this series can be used to inform debate, help develop critical thinking skills, increase global awareness, and enhance an understanding of international perspectives on history.

Material in each volume is selected from a diverse range of sources, including journals, magazines, newspapers, nonfiction books, personal narratives, speeches, congressional testimony, government documents, pamphlets, organization newsletters, and position papers. Articles taken from these sources are carefully edited and introduced to provide context and background. Each volume of Perspectives on Modern World History includes an array of views on events of global significance. Much of the material comes from international sources and from US sources that provide extensive international coverage.

Each volume in the Perspectives on Modern World History series also includes:

- A full-color **world map**, offering context and geographic perspective.
- An annotated **table of contents** that provides a brief summary of each essay in the volume.
- An **introduction** specific to the volume topic.
- For each viewpoint, a brief **introduction** that has notes about the author and source of the viewpoint, and that provides a summary of its main points.
- Full-color **charts**, **graphs**, **maps**, and other visual representations.

- Informational **sidebars** that explore the lives of key individuals, give background on historical events, or explain scientific or technical concepts.
- A **glossary** that defines key terms, as needed.
- A **chronology** of important dates preceding, during, and immediately following the event.
- A **bibliography** of additional books, periodicals, and Web sites for further research.
- A comprehensive **subject index** that offers access to people, places, and events cited in the text.

Perspectives on Modern World History is designed for a broad spectrum of readers who want to learn more about not only history but also current events, political science, government, international relations, and sociology—students doing research for class assignments or debates, teachers and faculty seeking to supplement course materials, and others wanting to improve their understanding of history. Each volume of Perspectives on Modern World History is designed to illuminate a complicated event, to spark debate, and to show the human perspective behind the world's most significant happenings of recent decades.

INTRODUCTION

In *Mein Kampf* (*My Struggle*), Adolf Hitler's biographic and political treatise, the aspiring dictator of Germany bared his misguided philosophy for social change in Europe. Writing in part during his incarceration in 1923 after a failed attempt to incite revolution in his homeland, Hitler envisioned a new Germany—a new Europe—that would not be under what he believed to be the financial control of a worldwide Jewish conspiracy. Painting his—and Germany's—enemy as the foulest and most deceptive social vermin, the future despot claimed rather assuredly that "no one need be surprised if among our people the personification of the devil as the symbol of all evil assumes the living shape of the Jew." Worse than simple economic dominance, the Jews, in Hitler's opinion, were bent on diluting the blood of the non-Jewish races in Europe by crossbreeding with supposedly pure Aryan people, to increase their hold on European society. Hitler informed his readership that "with every means [the Jew] tries to destroy the racial foundations of the people he has set out to subjugate," clearly promoting fears that Aryan women were not safe from the "lecherous" Jew. Several historians assert that even during these early years, when Hitler's rise to power was not assured, the would-be leader of Germany's Third Reich spoke of his plans to eliminate European Jewry if he could attain high office.

When, in the midst of political and economic turmoil in Germany, the German president, Paul von Hindenburg, appointed Hitler to the office of chancellor in 1933, the path was opened for the new executive to re-create the state. Immediately Hitler's National Socialist (Nazi) Party began drafting laws to remove Jews from positions of social importance—disbarring Jewish lawyers, forbidding Jewish doctors from treating non-Jewish patients, dispossessing Jewish farmers, and limiting the number of Jewish students entering universities. The following year, von Hindenburg died, and Hitler assumed total control of the German government. The Nazis then passed the Nuremberg Laws in 1935, disenfranchising most Jews and barring them from intermarrying with non-Jews in Germany.

Clearly, the Nazi plan of ousting Jews from Aryan society was at hand, and it is tempting to blame Hitler and his cronies for the rampant persecution that would lead to the greater evils of the Holocaust. However, as the US Holocaust Museum points out, although the decision to enact restrictive laws may have begun with the Nazi administration:

> State, regional, and municipal officials, on their own initiative, also promulgated a barrage of exclusionary decrees in their own communities. Thus, hundreds of individuals in all levels of government throughout the country were involved in the persecution of Jews as they conceived, discussed, drafted, adopted, enforced, and supported anti-Jewish legislation. No corner of Germany was left untouched.

This view, that the governmental hierarchy zealously took part in the expulsion of Jews from German life, suggests that anti-Jewish sentiments were rife across the Reich. Indeed, anti-Semitism was common throughout Europe, America, and other parts of the globe in the 1930s. When, for example, Jews began fleeing Germany, Austria, and other Nazi-annexed lands for safe haven in the United States, Britain, and Canada in the late years of the decade, nations such as Poland and Romania hoped that they too could convince their Jewish residents to take advantage of the great exodus. Unfortunately, the Western nations almost immediately contrived reasons that they could not increase their immigration quotas to accept all the Jewish refugees. Even more disturbing, various European nations witnessed anti-Jewish demonstrations in the years prior to the onset of war. As William I. Brustein writes in *Roots of Hate: Anti-Semitism in Europe before the Holocaust*, "By 1938, Germany and Austria did not stand alone in Europe in terms of the enactment of anti-Semitic laws. Anti-Semitic laws found a home in Bulgaria, Hungary, Poland, Romania, and Slovakia."

After Germany invaded and seized most of Poland in 1939 and the European war began, the Nazis were faced with a new problem: what to do with the Jews captured in foreign lands. Heinrich Himmler, the chief of the SS (Schutzstaffel) Nazi troops, appointed Reinhard Heydrich to head the Reich Main Security Office and tasked him with solving this problem. Heydrich began by utilizing the SS police and paramilitary units to round up and kill off many of the Polish intelligentsia and political activists—which included many Jews—and then corral large segments of the remaining Jewish populations into ghettos throughout major cities in Poland. In these cramped, walled-off sections where they were required to live, Jews were supposed to work for the German war effort. However, their ill treatment and forced starvation left no doubt that the SS plan of *Vernichtung durch Arbeit* (destruction through labor) was already in place even before the mass deportation of Jews to the infamous concentration camps.

About a year before Germany invaded Russia in June 1941, the Nazis established forced labor and extermination camps in Poland to deal mainly with Jews from both Germany and occupied countries that could not be packed into the already overcrowded ghettos. In Auschwitz, perhaps the most notorious of the concentration camps on Polish soil, Jews were divided into those who could work and those who could not. The former labored on German construction and armaments projects;

the latter were exterminated. Rudolf Höss, the commandant of the camp from 1940 to 1943, estimated that about three million Jews perished in Auschwitz (the figure has since been estimated down to just over one million).

Because more than 160,000 Jews were deported from Germany and others were starved, worked to death, or outright murdered within the Reich, historians have argued over how well-informed the average German was of the Nazis' "Final Solution" to the Jewish problem. Some claim the German people were ignorant of the tragedy; others maintain that the average German had to be cognizant of the horrors of the Holocaust because of the vast logistical organization needed for the enterprise. Hundreds of thousands of Jews would not simply relocate themselves out of their homes and homeland. Furthermore, given the degree of violence perpetrated against Jews before deportation began, many students of the Holocaust assume that the German people must have been aware that the fate of the Jews would not be mere imprisonment.

In a December 11, 2000, issue of *Idea* magazine, Evelin Gerda Lindner asserts that many Germans followed Hitler's commands because he told them what they wanted to hear: that Germany was not a weak nation after its defeat in World War I, and that the German people could regain their strength, their economy, and their identity, if they could only overcome the "Jewish conspiracy" that kept them humiliated. "Hitler ennobled the 'little people' by including them in the elite Germanic Aryan race with an important national mission," Lindner claims. Other historians agree that the German people were susceptible to Nazi propaganda and, like many patriotic citizens, assumed their leaders were steering the country in the right direction regardless of personal misgivings about the chosen path.

Other recent scholarship, however, does not absolve the ordinary German from blame so easily. In his 1996 book *Hitler's Willing Executioners: Ordinary Germans and the Holocaust*, Harvard professor Daniel J. Goldhagen insists that no amount of propaganda could convince average, thinking, feeling people that the Jews deserved to be rounded up, deported, and killed unless the belief already existed in their minds that the Jews were inferior and blameworthy. Goldhagen argues that the logistics of the Holocaust required the participation of so many average Germans that it becomes impossible to allege the innocence or naïveté of the general population. According to Goldhagen,

> The perpetrators, "ordinary Germans," were animated by anti-Semitism but by a particular *type* of anti-Semitism that led them to conclude that the Jews *ought to die*. The perpetrators' beliefs, their particular brand of anti-Semitism, though obviously not the sole source, was, I maintain, a most significant and indispensable source of the perpetrators' actions and must be at the center of any explanation of them. Simply put, the perpetrators, having consulted their own convictions and morality and having judged the mass annihilation of Jews to be right, did not *want* to say "no."

Goldhagen's theory has met with mixed reaction in scholarly circles. Few wish to concede that average Germans could be responsible for effecting, if not embracing, the Final Solution. Certainly some Germans resisted Nazi doctrine, and there are multiple stories of German citizens hiding Jews and laying their lives on the line to get German Jews to safety. However, Goldhagen's assertions are based on the type of virulent anti-Semitism that other authors have noted existed in Europe at the time. In *The Origins of the Final Solution: The Evolution of Nazi Jewish Policy, September 1939–March 1942*, Christopher R. Browning notes, for example, that the SS killing squads that followed the German army into Russia had help—especially in the Ukraine—from the local population in rounding up Jews in captured territories. A similar story is evident in the parts of France controlled by the pro-Nazi Vichy government set up in Southern France when that nation fell to German forces in 1940. Obviously, Adolf Hitler was not the only European to envision a new Europe free from the Jewish element.

Though it is easy to blame the Holocaust on entrenched continental attitudes (whether specifically Nazi or broadly European), historians have also not let the Allied nations escape accusation of abetting the murder of the Jews. In 2001, documents released from the US National Archives suggest that foreign diplomats alerted the Allies to the large-scale deportation of Jews as early as November 1941. By the following year, British intelligence had picked up coded messages that hinted at genocide, but the information was fragmentary. In a 2005 report called "Eavesdropping on Hell," US National Security Agency historian Robert J. Hanyok stated that, "Topics of enormous importance to understanding the Holocaust, such as the depredations of the police and SS units in Russia, the operations of the death camps, and the roundup of the Hungarian Jews, barely were mentioned in the extant material." Throughout 1942, the US Foreign Office and other parts of the government received communications from trustworthy individuals who documented incidence of brutality and murder, yet these scraps of information were not acted upon. President Franklin D. Roosevelt joined other Allied leaders in issuing a warning to Germany that condemned the "bestial policy of cold-blooded extermination" of European Jews. Critics who believe the Allies could have done more to save the Jews fault Roosevelt for not pressing the Allies to head for known concentration camps when US and British troops finally joined the Russians in collapsing Hitler's Fortress Europe. The president's defenders counter that Roosevelt believed the best way to help

European Jews was to swiftly end the war—which meant pursuing military and governmental targets.

Pinpointing responsibility for the tragedy that was the Holocaust is an ongoing endeavor that shows no signs of stopping. In September 2010, Pope Benedict XVI stated that atheism in Nazi Germany was the linchpin that secured the Jews' fate. This statement came only months after the Vatican was confronted by Jewish religious leaders who wanted the pope to address why Pope Pius XII, the spiritual patriarch during World War II, had failed to issue any indictment against Germany for its persecution of the Jews. In 2005 German chancellor Gerard Schröder visited the Auschwitz memorial and spoke chilling words that must have resonated with the German public. "The evil of the Nazi ideology did not come out of nowhere. The brutalisation of thought and the lack of moral inhibitions had a history," the *Guardian* (UK) newspaper reported Schröder saying. "One thing is clear: The Nazi ideology was willed by people and carried out by people."

While Schröder was perhaps finally voicing Germany's war guilt, it is more significant to note that the chancellor laid the blame at the feet of people—complex human beings whose motivations are cast from a variety of molds. This is why Holocaust survivors and commemorators encourage new generations across the globe to "never forget" the horrors that took place. As survivor and author Elie Wiesel exhorted in the preface to his Holocaust memoir *Night*:

> For the survivor who chooses to testify, it is clear: his duty is to bear witness for the dead and the living. He has no right to deprive future generations of a past that belongs to our collective memory. To forget would be not only dangerous but offensive; to forget the dead would be akin to killing them a second time. The witness has forced himself to testify. For the youth of today,

for the children who will be born tomorrow. He does not want his past to become their future.

For Wiesel, everyone must be reminded—and it is the duty of those who survive great tragedies to remind the world—that human beings are capable of great evil and that only through constant vigilance and remembrance will the horrors of the past not be visited upon future generations.

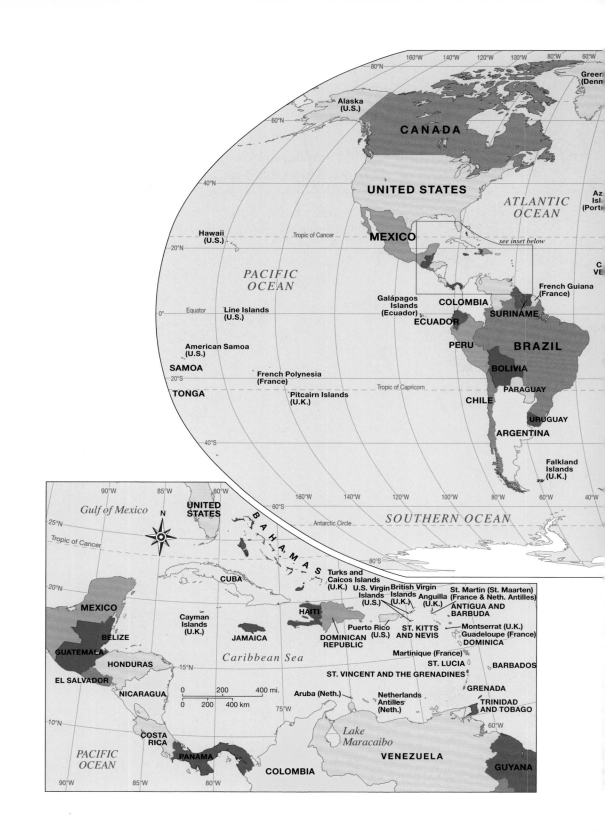

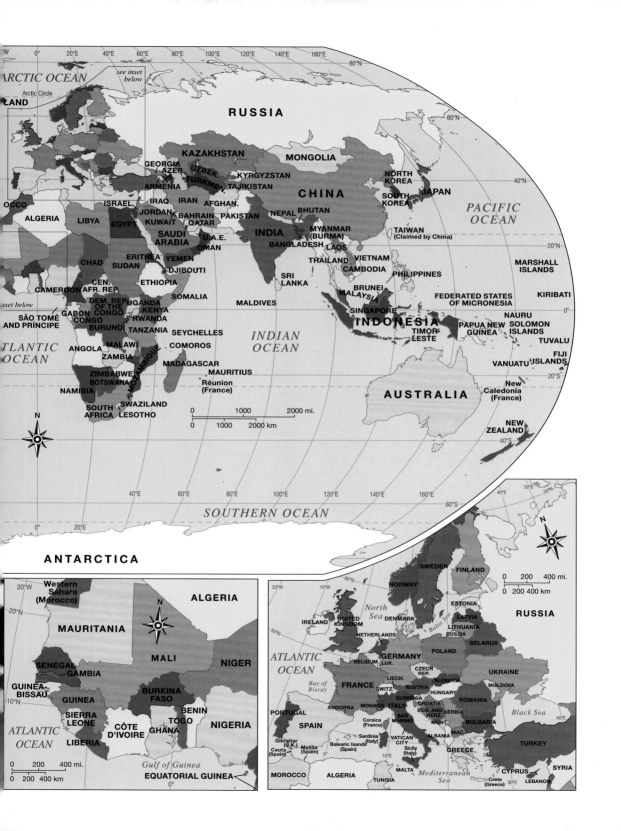

CHAPTER 1

Historical Background on the Holocaust

An Overview of the Holocaust

Gregory Paul Wegner

Gregory Paul Wegner provides a straightforward overview of the origins and outcomes of the Holocaust in the following viewpoint. Wegner claims the mass exterminations that took place in Nazi Germany were aimed at ridding the country of undesirables and purifying the blood of the Aryan people. To this end, the Nazis first rounded up the disabled, the infirm, and the mentally ill and then broadened the scope of the atrocities to include political prisoners, religious dissidents, prisoners of war, and Jews. Focusing on the more than 5 million Jewish victims of Adolf Hitler's Final Solution, Wegner explains that several historians claim that the genocide of European Jewry did not result from some master plan that had been well thought out before the Nazis' rise to power. These researchers insist that the Holocaust had roots in anti-Semitic feelings that pervaded Europe and had played out in Germany through various attempts

Photo on previous page: In *Mein Kampf* (*My Struggle*), Adolf Hitler expresses his vision of a Europe under German dominance and without Jews. (**AFP/Getty Images.**)

SOURCE. Gregory Paul Wegner, "Holocaust," *Macmillan Encyclopedia of Death and Dying.* Edited by Robert Kastenbaum. Copyright © Gale, a part of Cengage Learning, Inc. Reproduced by permission. www.cengage.com/permissions.

to bar, persecute, and even deport Jews from the Aryan lands that Hitler conceived of as Germany's Third Reich, the newest empire that would dominate Europe. Wegner seems to agree that the punitive laws, concentration camps, and mobile killing squads were part of a patchwork solution to the "Jewish problem" and were devised piecemeal in conjunction with an ever-expanding war against Allied armies. Wegner is an educational historian whose work has focused on Nazi Germany. His most recent book is *Anti-Semitism and Schooling under the Third Reich*.

Historians and social scientists still struggle to understand how a country with one of the highest literacy rates in the world and a culture which nurtured great scientists, musicians, and theologians could administer one of the biggest mass murders in history, carried out with the complicity of millions and with the aid of the most modern technological means available. Indeed, the Germans were to industrialize mass death and the disposal of their remains. Germany was not the only country with a culture marked by deep-seated anti-Semitic resentments, but it was the only one to transform this resentment into a policy directed toward annihilating the entire Jewish people.

Neither were the Jews the only group identified for total destruction because of racial reasons. The infamous "T-4" killings of the handicapped, the mentally ill, and those suffering from hereditary illness conducted by medical doctors under [Nazi Germany's leader Adolf] Hitler's orders preceded the formation of the death camps in the East. These were the first victims of mass murder. Under the guise of "euthanasia" and supported by the legal apparatus of the state, as many as 6,000 children and 70,273 adults met their deaths at the hands of medical professionals in asylums across the [Third] Reich. The vast majority of the victims died in gas chambers. The choice of method for this kind of murder was critically important for the future. The early Nazi elimination of "life unworthy of life" through the "T-4" killings foreshadowed the use of gas chambers in Auschwitz and other camps as well. Both the technology and many of the former medical personnel from this sordid experiment in mass murder would re-emerge with the SS [Nazi troops], or *schutzstaffel*, in helping to run the machinery of the death camps after 1941. The story did not end here. The intent to racially cleanse Germany of undesirable racial elements also extended to Sinti and Roma, called *Zigeuner* by the Germans and known traditionally as "Gypsies." Classified by the Nazis as "criminal" or "asocials" and forced to wear the black triangle on prisoner clothing, at least 250,000 Sinti and Roma died under Nazi rule. Whether the Nazis fully intended to wipe out the entire population of Sinti and Roma remains an issue of some dispute among scholars.

The Road to Auschwitz

There existed no doubt among Nazi policymakers regarding the scope of mass murder and the massive destruction of Jews in the wake of the attack on Russia in the summer of 1941. The Nazi intention was to kill every single Jewish man, woman, and child. Hitler vented his obsessive hatred for Jews in *Mein Kampf* (*My Struggle*), originally written in Landsberg prison in 1924. The Jewish community stood in diametric opposition to his racial vision for a New Germany. Judeophobia, as the scholar Klaus Fischer calls it, reflected a paranoid distortion of reality and delusionary thinking. After rising to power in 1933, Hitler wasted little time before moving against the Jews and other avowed enemies of the state. Dachau, the first of many concentration camps originally created to

> The mass murder of Jews and others declared unworthy of citizenship did not take place overnight.

incarcerate political enemies of the regime, opened less than two months after Hitler came to office. The SA, or *sturmabteilung*, brown-shirted storm troopers, rounded up Social Democrats and Communists. The Nazis followed on April 1, 1933, by boycotting all Jewish businesses. Even more devastating to the Jewish community was the dismissal of all Jews from civil service and the legal practice six days later.

The mass murder of Jews and others declared unworthy of citizenship did not take place overnight. State violence and terror, in order to be more fully institutionalized, required the legitimacy of a legal framework. Early on the perpetrators created a series of laws to legalize the oppressive actions taken against their victims. Compulsory sterilization laws appeared in July 1933 leading to the forced sterilization of over 320,000 people suffering from hereditary illnesses. Forced to wear the pink triangle and condemned under Paragraph 175 of the 1871 Reich Criminal Code, which made homosexual relations a criminal offense, at least 10,000 gays suffered imprisonment and deplorable treatment in at least eleven concentration camps.

The legal noose continued to tighten around the Jews. A public book-burning of works by Jewish authors like Heinrich Heine and Sigmund Freud along with other opponents of Nazism took place in May 1933. Signs declaring "No Jews" sprung up all over the country during the summer of 1935 outside restaurants, stores, and villages forbidding Jewish entry. A critically important racial development emerged in September of that year under the anti-Semitic Nuremberg Laws. These laws virtually stripped Jews of citizenship, legitimizing the huge social chasm between Jews and Aryan Germans. With the intent of preserving blood purity, Jews could not marry and have sexual relations with Germans or employ female employees under the age of forty-five in their households.

The World Waits and Watches

An equally ominous but perhaps lesser known aspect of the Holocaust regarded early reactions of the global community to the treatment of the Jews. At an international conference staged at Evian in France during early July 1938, diplomats representing thirty-two nations met to discuss solutions in answer to a growing refugee problem. The mounting number of Jewish refugees from Austria and Germany created pressure on the United States and other countries to raise immigration quotas. Little more than expressions of sympathy for the Jews

An eternal flame burns at the Holocaust Memorial Center in Farmington Hills, MI, to commemorate the millions of lives lost during the Holocaust. (**Associated Press.**)

came out of the conference. In short, the conference results convinced Hitler that "no one wanted the Jews" and, moreover, implied that he had a free hand in dealing with the Jews without international interference.

A growing escalation of violence against the Jews occurred during *Kristallnacht,* or the Night of the Broken Glass, on November 9, 1938. That evening, over 1,000 synagogues across Austria and Germany were burned and many Jewish businesses looted and destroyed. Ninety-six Jews were murdered and 30,000 were arrested and sent to concentration camps in Dachau, Sachsenhausen, and Buchenwald. Eight days later, Jewish children were expelled from German schools. Economic pressures increased; the isolation of the Jews continued with the compulsory expropriation of their businesses, industries, and shops with the "Aryanization" of the economy in December of that year.

The Final Solution, the Nazi answer to the Jewish question, did not follow a direct path from Hitler's obsessive hatred of Jews, as expressed in *Mein Kampf,* to the killing fields of the death camps. A major focus of Nazi policy from 1933 to 1941 was to use forced emigration to clear Germany of all Jews. At least as late as the closing days of 1938, the Nazi regime explored the possibility of organizing a wholesale migration of Jews to either Madagascar or Palestine. Some historians, like Gerald Fleming and Eberhard Jäckel, known in some quarters as intentionalists, claim a direct connection between Hitler's anti-Semitic ideology and anti-Semitic practices. Karl Schleunes, representing a more functionalist point of view, argues that the Nazi leadership from the top down had not defined the scope and substance of the Final Solution.

> Death camps, of which there were six in number, were located in Poland. Their sole purpose was to kill as many Jews as quickly as possible.

Conditions of the war on the eastern front marked a critical phase in the Holocaust. Vast tracts of territory, along with huge numbers of Russian prisoners of war and Jews, fell under German control during the early phase of Hitler's war with Russia. [American Holocaust historian] Christopher Browning's research argues convincingly that Hitler gave the go ahead for the mass murder of the Jews in the fall of 1941, some four months after Germany attacked Russia. This distinction is important since it sheds new light on the old and misguided assumption that plans for the Final Solution were first instituted months later as part of the Wannsee Conference on January 20, 1942. Knowing when Hitler and his circle passed the point of no return in regard to killing Jews remains important for students of the Holocaust for several reasons. As Browning reminds readers, this extreme case of genocide was different from other genocides in that the goal was to eliminate every single Jewish person in the entire Reich and occupied territories. This genocide remains unique as a turning point in history for another reason. The Nazi regime exploited the latest technology as well as considerable bureaucratic and scientific resources to achieve the most thorough and efficient killing process possible.

The Dynamics of Nazi Mass Murder

An important distinction existed between the formation of concentration as opposed to death camps within the Nazi racial state. Concentration camps originally imprisoned political opponents. Eventually, as racial enemies of the regime, Jews also became part of the prison population in the concentration camps. Death camps, of which there were six in number, were located in Poland. Their sole purpose was to kill as many Jews as quickly as possible. Auschwitz, Chelmno, Treblinka, Sobibor, Maidanek, and Belzec are places that will forever live in the memory of the Holocaust. Of these, Auschwitz was by far the largest. From at least 1.3 million deportees to Auschwitz, about 900,000 met their end very soon after arrival. Another 400,000 entered as camp prisoners and [were] given identification numbers. About half of these people died of disease, hunger, or slave labor. Many of the remainder met their end by injection, medical experiments, or the gas chambers. Ninety percent of the victims in Auschwitz were Jews. Poles constituted the second largest group followed by Gypsies and Soviet prisoners of war.

The geographical location of the death camps in the East afforded a certain level of official secrecy and deceit in the administration of mass murder. The six camps were located close to the highest concentration of Jews in all of Europe. Prewar Poland had a Jewish population of just less than 3 million. Auschwitz, which opened its gates as a death camp in 1942, was favorably situated because of its location at a confluence of major railroad lines. The railroads acted as major arteries to the death camps running from all parts of occupied Europe. Day and night Jews from twenty countries were shipped to their deaths.

The railroads, in order to operate as efficiently as possible, relied on armies of trusted bureaucrats who, with the stroke of their pens, determined the fate of hundreds of thousands of people. These same faceless figures rarely witnessed the lethal results of their orders. SS Officer Adolf Eichmann, as master bureaucrat, was a central figure in this process since he designed and administered the entire transportation system for the purpose of speeding up the process of mass murder. The memoirs of Rudolf Höss, SS commandant of Auschwitz, reveal a kind and dedicated family man who felt no hatred for Jews. In the banal language of the brutally efficient bureaucrat, he simply had a job to do.

The power of Nazi propaganda to work a language of deceit was an important factor in efficiently moving large groups of people to their unknown destinations.

TOTAL DEATHS FROM NAZI GENOCIDAL POLICIES	
Group	**Deaths**
European Jews	5,600,000 to 6,250,000
Soviet prisoners of war	3,000,000
Polish Catholics	3,000,000
Serbians	700,000
Roma, Sinti, and Lalleri [Gypsies]	222,000 to 250,000
Germans (political, religious, and Resistance)	80,000
Germans (handicapped)	70,000
Homosexuals	12,000
Jehovah's Witnesses	2,500

Source: John Roth, *The Holocaust Chronicle: A History in Words and Pictures*. Chicago: Publications International, 2000.

Victims were packed into cattle cars under the most inhumane conditions without food, water, or basic sanitation. To quell the threat of riots, Nazi officials informed passengers that they were part of a resettlement project. Showers, clean clothing, and hot soup were among those things promised at journey's end. Jewish musicians were pressed into service to play classical music at the gate of Auschwitz to soothe the anxieties of incoming prisoners. The real truth of the matter was hidden in an intricate language of deception. To make the situation even more precarious, Jews were required by law to wear the yellow star in September 1941. The Nazis developed no less than twenty-five expressions to mask the real meaning behind mass murder. *Sonderbehandlung* conveyed a literal meaning of special treatment. The expression really meant taking Jews through the death process in the camp. Arriving prisoners saw a welcome sign for *Badeanstalten*, or bath houses, which really were gas chambers.

Not all Jews were killed in the camps. To facilitate the killing operations, the Germans initiated the *Einsatzgruppen*, or mobile killing squads under the direction of the SS. This newly formed "police army" swept through areas newly conquered by the German army in Poland and Russia. Thousands of Jewish women and children were hunted down and shot on the spot. Males were either executed or deported. This massive killing campaign, carried out primarily in 1942, demonstrated the highly concentrated methods used by the SS to eliminate as many people as possible within a relatively short timeframe. This was another face of the Holocaust which reflected the serious Nazi intent and purpose to carry out a war against the Jews.

> Exactly how many victims died in the Holocaust will never be known with great exactitude.

The Accounting of Death

Exactly how many victims died in the Holocaust will never be known with great exactitude. Six million Jews lost their lives under the Nazi regime, a figure most commonly cited over the years by historians and social scientists. This statistical assumption continues to come under scrutiny. The historian Gerald Fleming argues with certainty that the figure reaches the 5 million mark. Raoul Hilberg proposes a slightly higher number of Jewish victims at 5.1 million. One important basis for determining the scope of human destruction in the death camps are the railroad passenger numbers and points of departure with dates carefully documented by the SS. While the toll of other twentieth-century disasters are often known to the single person, the loss of life from the Holocaust can only be estimated to within hundreds of thousands and millions. In some cases, entire Jewish communities in eastern Europe were wiped off the face of the earth.

More Competing Views

Noted earlier were the competing views of scholars regarding the intentional versus the functional nature of Nazi ideology and the Holocaust. Another voice, which emerged in the mid-1990s, sparked a firestorm of debate. Daniel Goldhagen's *Hitler's Willing Executioners* (1996) claims that anti-Semitic hatred, nurtured in the soil of Christianity, was *the* central cause for the Holocaust and that such hatred was imbedded in German culture. Goldhagen attacks the cherished assumption that Germans were guilty only of obedience to authority. Like many other institutions under the fascist process of centralization, the churches participated in an already deeply rooted German tendency toward "eliminationist anti-Semitism."

> The emergence of Holocaust denial as a cultural phenomenon, often reflecting an anti-Semitic agenda from elements of the Far Right, is not one to be overlooked or easily dismissed.

Goldhagen's thesis came under withering criticism by a host of historians. The prominent German historian Eberhard Jäckel accused Goldhagen of advancing "primitive stereotypes" while making wholly inaccurate contrasts between anti-Semitism in Germany and developments in Italy and Denmark. Christopher Browning's scholarship emphasizes obedience to authority as a critical development leading to the Holocaust. He carefully contends that the demonization of an entire people with the charge of anti-Semitism explains nothing. Goldhagen's reductionist argument did not sit well among many historians. The controversial nature of the Holocaust, deeply embroiled in the causes and motivations for mass murder, promises new and expanded debates in the future.

Appearing in the late twentieth century, certain revisionist historians like David Irving and Arthur Butz, members of the infamous Institute for Historical Review, exploited historical ignorance and nascent anti-Semitic prejudices by denying the Holocaust. Irving had long argued that Hitler remained ignorant of the Holocaust and Butz insisted that gas chambers did not exist at Auschwitz. The emergence of Holocaust denial as a cultural phenomenon, often reflecting an anti-Semitic agenda from elements of the Far Right, is not one to be overlooked or easily dismissed. A legal confrontation was inevitable. In 2000 a civil trial in London, where Irving sued the scholar Deborah Lipstadt for calling him a Holocaust denier, ended in disgrace for the plaintiff and a resounding public condemnation of Irving's historical claims about Hitler and the Jews by the judge. The controversy is not over. The language of anti-Semitic hatred continues to find audiences on the Internet under a growing number of web sites. In the Federal Republic of Germany and Canada, public denials of the Holocaust are considered expressions of hate language, incitements to violence, and insults to the dead. As such, these actions are considered serious violations of federal law in both nations.

A Tragedy That Still Resonates Today

The long shadow of the Holocaust continues to shape world affairs. The tremendous sorrow, grief, and sense of betrayal from the Holocaust provided a powerful emotional and political thrust for Jews to create the state of Israel in 1948. Research protocols ensuring the protection of research subjects, growing out of the revelations of the Nuremberg trials, influences the way research is conducted today. Millions each year visit the extensive exhibits in the Holocaust and Memorial Museum in Washington, D.C. A new memorial in the center of Berlin, finalized after a protracted debate in the Federal Republic, will memorialize millions of Jews whose lives were lost in one of the most horrendous genocides in human history. The legal settlements over Swiss gold, which began in 1998 and continue into the twenty-first century, as well as reparations paid by German corporations who employed forced laborers, raised a new awareness about the complicity of economic interests in the Nazi exploitation of minority populations. A deeper understanding about the human capacity for evil is an inescapable part of this legacy.

The Nazi Party Secures Power in Germany

Economist

The National Socialist—"Nazi"—Party began its ascension in Germany just after World War I when the nation was humiliated by the defeat it suffered at the hands of the Allies—the United Kingdom, France, and Russia. Basing its doctrine on an opposition to Marxism, a virulent anti-Semitism, and faith in a pan-Germanic Third Reich, the party rose to power by proclaiming a resurrection of German strength. By 1933, German president Paul von Hindenburg gave in to pressure and appointed Nazi leader Adolf Hitler as Germany's new chancellor. In the following viewpoint, a correspondent for the *Economist*, a British newspaper that does not use author bylines so that the journal can speak with a unified voice, describes how the Nazi Party used its showmanship—parades, speeches, rallies, propaganda—to spread its ideology and entrance millions of Germans who were dispirited in the interwar years. The author warns that the Nazi Party's tactics have been successful at hypnotizing the masses, and he expects that their caustic and hate-filled doctrines will

SOURCE. "Revolutionary Germany—I," *Economist*, July 8, 1933, pp. 63–64. Copyright © 1933 by Economist Newspaper Group. Reproduced with permission of Economist Newspaper Group.

win out if Hitler can give the people back a thriving economy and ample comforts in addition to stirring, nationalistic rhetoric.

*P*anem et Circenses [bread and circuses] was the old Roman recipe for doping the people. The National Socialist [Nazi] revolution in Germany has started with circuses, and it is to be hoped that the bread will follow. The first circus was a terror, directed against those whom the Revolution considered to be the root of all evil—Marxists, pacifists, internationalists and Jews. It seemed on the whole fairly moderate in comparison with the excesses of other great revolutions. But although the German revolution is certainly great, absolute power was gained without firing a shot. On the surface the terror, which was very real, thus appeared utterly unnecessary.

Nazis are apt to claim that the excesses were spontaneous outbreaks from below. This is, however, more than debatable. [Nazi Cabinet minister] Captain [Hermann] Göring made a speech in which he expressly said that every bullet fired by the storm troops and the police was his bullet, and this speech was a signal for many excesses. He can therefore scarcely disclaim responsibility. Indeed, it is foolish for Nazi leaders to do so. From their point of view, according to which the ends justifies the means, and the rights of the individual are as nothing compared with the good of the community as interpreted by themselves, there were two important reasons for the terror. In the first place, a revolutionary army which has suffered from persecution, which has been taught that certain sections of the community are more or less fiends incarnate, which has been led to expect that "heads will roll in the sand" when the revolution takes place, might quite conceivably turn on its leaders unless given its head (and another head or two!) at any rate for a time. It was given its head, but only to a limited extent. A young East

Adolf Hitler Consolidates Power in Germany

[Adolf Hitler's] first 2 years in office [as German chancellor] were almost wholly dedicated to the consolidation of power. With several prominent Nazis in key positions (Hermann Göring, as minister of interior in Prussia, and Wilhelm Frick, as minister of interior of the central government, controlled the police forces) and his military ally Werner von Blomberg in the Defense Ministry, [Hitler] quickly gained practical control. He persuaded the aging president and the Reichstag [German parliament] to invest him with emergency powers suspending the constitution in the so-called Enabling Act of Feb. 28, 1933. Under this act and with the help of a mysterious fire in the Reichstag building, he rapidly eliminated his political rivals and brought all levels of government and major political institutions under his control. By means of the Roehm purge of the summer of 1934 [when Hitler had military leader Ernst Roehm executed to stave off

a military coup] he assured himself of the loyalty of the army by the subordination of the Nazi storm troopers and the murder of its chief together with the liquidation of major rivals within the army. The death of President [Paul von] Hindenburg in August 1934 cleared the way for the abolition of the presidential title by plebiscite [vote]. Hitler became officially Führer of Germany and thereby head of state as well as commander in chief of the armed forces. [Minister of Propaganda] Joseph Goebbels's extensive propaganda machine and [leader of the SS Nazi forces] Heinrich Himmler's police system simultaneously perfected totalitarian control of Germany, as demonstrated most impressively in the great Nazi mass rally of 1934 in Nuremberg, where millions marched in unison and saluted Hitler's theatrical appeals.

SOURCE. *"Adolf Hitler,"* Encyclopedia of World Biography. *Vol. 7. 2nd ed. Detroit: Gale, 2004.*

Prussian storm troop leader, a fine physical type and in many respects capable of intelligent argument, told the writer that only severe discipline prevented an absolute pogrom.

The Nazis Control Every German Organization

In the second place, the terror broke down the psychological resistance of the individual. Whether or not it was deliberately intended, this factor has been of immense importance in carrying out the so-called *Gleichschaltung* or "co-ordination" of the nation. This catchword was derived from the "Co-ordination Law" which gave the Nazis control of all organs of local government. The process has eliminated Jews and other inconvenient persons from key positions and has given the Nazis control or at any rate a predominant position in practically every organisation in the country, from skittle clubs to industrial associations. The disadvantages, indeed the impossibility, of legislation to this end are obvious. But stories of bodies found in the Grünewald [forest in Berlin] greatly expedited negotiations conducted, and the signature of letters of resignation presented, by armed gentlemen in brown shirts [Adolf Hitler's paramilitary followers]. It soon became unnecessary to send the gentlemen at all.

This particular "circus" has served its turn, and its tents are being folded and stowed. For the last month [June 1933] the Nazi leaders have been using every effort to stop individual actions of the kind described. Storm troopers making unauthorised arrests and Nazi Commissioners continuing the process of "co-ordination" without official authority are liable to find themselves in jail or at any rate excluded from the party. Such action against members of the party does not, it is true, get reported in the Press. The leaders naturally do not want to discredit the party, and this is probably one of the reasons why special secret legal procedure on military lines has been introduced for the

> Although discipline is being asserted [in Germany under Nazi rule], there is a secret State police . . . , imprisonment without trial is common, and no opponent of the régime can sleep quietly in his bed.

storm troops. But although discipline is being asserted, there is a secret State police reminiscent of the Ogpu [Soviet Union's secret police until 1934], imprisonment without trial is common, and no opponent of the régime can sleep quietly in his bed.

Perfecting the Machinery of the Nazi State

As an aid to the maintenance of discipline, members of the party are being given plenty to do. There are continual processions, fêtes, marches, meetings, speeches, another form of "circus." The writer was cordially invited to take part in a number of them, got up by relatively small party organisations. The Nazis are proud of their machine, of their enthusiasm, of the spirit, which inspires them, and are anxious to show it off. It cannot be denied that there is good reason for their pride. There is a great deal of idealism and a truly corporate spirit. Every member is addressed as "Party Comrade," whether he be a duke or a dustman. There is no kow-towing to social rank. Everyone begins at the bottom, and is expected to work under the orders of his immediate superior in the party hierarchy. In a speech the other day the leader of a "district" comprising 20,000 members, in private life a commercial traveller, said that he would expect a new member, however eminent (for example, a leading permanent official) to write out chits or act as messenger for two hours every Sunday. He explained that it would be a good rest from brainwork. And this sort of thing is done. There are no committees; the principle of leadership is supreme, and the immediate superior of an industrial magnate may be a simple workman. In this way, so Hitler believes, the workers can be given back their self-respect and induced to abandon the idea of class warfare. But it is not clear what ends this militant hierarchy will serve once the "State" is perfected.

Photo on following page: Events such as this 1933 Berlin funeral procession for a slain Nazi helped unify the party and thus cement its control over Germany. (**Associated Press.**)

Many of the party celebrations are, of course, definitely Nationalist in character. The tenth anniversary of [German officer Albert Leo] Schlageter's execution by the French in the Ruhr[1] was the signal for a great many. The writer was a guest at the unveiling of a Schlageter memorial followed by a torchlight procession. Considering the occasion, the speeches were not incendiary, although they somewhat naturally harped on Germany's degradation in those days. Only one speaker mentioned the possibility of a war of liberation. The best speech was that made by the Senior Nazi, a member of the Reichstag [German parliament], who took as his theme the fact that Schlageter was betrayed by his own countrymen. Our aim is not war, he said, but national unity, self-respect, and the inspiration of all our countrymen with the ideals of sacrifice exemplified in Schlageter himself. It was subsequently remarked to the writer that it was regarded as a tragedy for Germany that it should be necessary to hammer patriotism into the heads of her citizens. In England, said my informant, patriotism is innate, but he used that rather discredited phrase, "my country, right or wrong," to prove it.

> Questions of national policy, of international right and wrong are only for the leader to decide; the individual's job is to stick up for his country and obey orders.

Faith in a New Creed, a New Leader

We in England cannot disclaim responsibility, for this saying is constantly on Nazi lips, and exactly hits off the spirit which is being installed into sixty-five million Germans to-day. It is not precisely an aggressive spirit; it is rather the idea that questions of national policy, of international right and wrong are only for the leader to decide; the individual's job is to stick up for his country and obey orders. It is not incompatible with peace, provided the leadership is peaceful, but it is the antithesis of pacifism. The Nazis are out to make sure that Germans will fight if called upon to do so. It may well be that to beat the patriotic drum in this way is the best way of getting rid of class antagonism. Hitler certainly thinks so. Man is unfortunately a combative animal, and if the workman is to give up fighting the capitalist, and *vice versa*, animosity has to be directed to other quarters. Put in a more favourable light, perhaps the best way to get rid of mere class solidarity and loyalty is to substitute national solidarity and loyalty. Yet one fact is worth noting. The Nazis do not merely adopt the "Damn the foreigner" attitude of most Jingoes in England. With one accord they regard National Socialism as a new creed which they hope and believe will sweep the world. It is something of a novelty for the Nationalist to want to make other nations nationalistic and therefore strong as well.

> With one accord [Nazis] regard National Socialism as a new creed which they hope and believe will sweep the world.

The third important form of circus is corruption hunting. Undoubtedly there was a fair amount of corruption in public and business life, and reaction to this in Germany is much the same as that in America, only more violent. The Nazi Economic Commissioner, Herr [Mr. Otto] Wagener, himself recounts that when he wanted to call the industrial leaders together to discuss his plans he found three hundred of them in jail. His first job, therefore, was to get a sufficient number of them out. Denunciations flowed thick and fast, and were usually followed by arrests. At the present time the Government and the party leaders are undoubtedly trying to put a stop to this evil, while continuing to give the impression of a general clean-up. Most significant is the tax amnesty for those who make a free gift to the Exchequer up to at least 50 per cent of their overdue payments. People with uneasy consciences can thus regain peace of mind and start afresh. This is certainly a wise move, since although the construction of prisons to house Germans who have not paid their taxes in full might stimulate the building industry, it is difficult to see how the business of the country could get along without them.

Circuses play their part in every revolution, and the Nazis are certainly past masters in the art of staging them. Germany to-day is an amazing example of mass hypnotism, indeed of mass enthusiasm. But hypnotism wears off, and enthusiasm cools, though the example of Russia shows that both can be kept alive for considerable periods. Hitler has asked for four years to produce bread. While it would be unwise to predict his fall, even if he fails, his position would at any rate be unenviable.

Note

1. Albert Leo Schlageter was a member of a proto-Nazi organization that resisted the French military occupation of the Ruhr valley after World War I. With confederates, he sabotaged French trains bringing supplies to military units in the region. He was caught and executed by French authorities and subsequently became a martyr to the Nazi Party.

Kristallnacht Signals the Beginning of Large-Scale Violence Against Jews in Germany

New York Times

In the following viewpoint, reporters from the *New York Times* and wireless news services report on the events of November 10, 1938. That day, anti-Jewish rioters took to the streets in Munich and several other German cities to loot and destroy Jewish-owned businesses and to evict Jewish tenants and merchants, supposedly to avenge the death of Ernst vom Rath, a German diplomat assassinated by a young Jew in Paris. In the ensuing pogrom, so many shop windows were broken that the event became known as Kristallnacht, "the night of broken glass." As the news services explain, German police sometimes protected Jews from physical harm, but officials also rounded up more than twenty-five thousand Jews (including prominent business and community leaders) and sent them to concentration camps. Documents also testify that the police were ordered to seize Jewish records and to not interfere with the rioting unless it endangered non-Jewish property. The open hostility and destruction during Kristallnacht made clear to German Jews that they were no longer welcome in the Nazi state.

All Jewish families were ordered this morning [November 10, 1938] to leave Munich within forty-eight hours and were instructed to inform the political police by 6 P.M. when they would hand over the keys to their dwellings and garages.

Instructions were issued to confiscate all Jewish-owned cars and the sale of gasoline to Jews was forbidden. In some cases Jews were told that they must leave Germany and they were forced to sign a statement to this effect. No notice was taken of the objection that most Jews were without passports. The only Jews with passports are those who have already made preparations to emigrate.

> Kauffingerstrasse, one of Munich's main streets, looked as if it had been raided by a bombing plane.

The news of the death of Ernst vom Rath [a German diplomat who was assassinated by a Jewish youth] in Paris was the signal for a reign of terror for the Jewish community in Munich, which began with the wrecking of shops during the night and continued with incendiarism during the morning and wholesale arrests and notices of expulsions during the day.

Crowds Fill Main Streets

Large crowds filled the main streets this morning to gaze on the destruction wrought in last night's riots, the full extent of which was visible only by daylight. Kauffinger-strasse, one of Munich's main streets, looked as if it had been raided by a bombing plane. A half-dozen of the best shops were converted into wreckage overnight with plate-glass windows splintered on the pavement, shelves torn down and goods lying broken and trampled on the floor.

So far as can be gathered every Jewish-owned shop in town was completely or partly wrecked as well as several "Aryan" businesses, which shared the general fate for having previously belonged to Jews.

An orthodox synagogue was set on fire early this morning; the alarm was raised about 8 A.M. but the flames caused much havoc before they could be controlled. The synagogue was reduced to a shell and the Jewish school adjoining it was also completely burned. It was reported that synagogues in Bernberg, Baireuth and Treutlingen were also burned.

Arrests of male Jews began at their homes at an early hour. It was estimated that so far about 400 had been taken into custody and also a half dozen women.

The windows of the well-known banking house of H. Aufhaeuser were stoned last night and this morning a Nazi commissar took control of the business which was already in the process of being "Aryanized." Aufhaeuser is one of Germany's most important banking concerns. Martin Aufhaeuser, the senior partner, was arrested. Another partner, Emil Kramer and his wife killed themselves at their home today.

The home of Karl Bach, a wealthy manufacturer who was arrested today, was set on fire last night. Among other prominent Jews taken into custody were three well-known surgeons, Professor Alfred Haas and Dr. Josef Rosenbaum (both of them had received permits to go to England) and Dr. M. Klar, Munich's leading orthopedic surgeon. Some Jews escaped arrest by remaining away from their homes and offices.

Frankfort Synagogues Burned

Wireless to *The New York Times.*

Since an early hour today anti-Jewish demonstrations and attacks against Jewish-owned property have occurred here as well as in many other places in Southwestern Germany.

All Jewish-owned shops, cafes and restaurants were demolished here apparently without exception. Four synagogues—and possibly more—were set on fire. A large synagogue on the Promenade was seriously damaged when it burned, but the walls and roof still stand. Another large synagogue in the neighborhood of the old Rothschild family [a German Jewish banking family] house in the ancient ghetto burned the entire morning, but the flames were finally extinguished about noon. The Rothschild house itself— a fine, medieval building—was not attacked, evidently because it is a museum now belonging to the city. A synagogue in the fashionable west end was totally destroyed.

The chief synagogue situated in the old ghetto near the world-famous ancient Jewish cemetery was also burned this morning and this afternoon and is a total wreck. The incendiarism also included Jewish-owned shops and houses and fire brigades from neighboring towns and villages had to be called to assist in fighting all these fires.

Demonstrators assembled outside Jewish houses all day. They smashed windows and in many cases penetrated the homes.

The police came with motorbuses, taking the Jews into "protective custody"—a measure no doubt necessary in view of the demonstrators' fury.

The aggressors, however, seem to have refrained from bodily attacks. They let the Jews alone but smashed their property.

> " Demonstrators assembled outside Jewish houses all day. They smashed windows and in many cases penetrated the homes. "

The Jewish-owned Hotel Ullman, in the center of the city, was attacked, many windows were smashed and furniture was thrown into the street.

The shops of a few American Jews residing here bore posters saying "American business" on the windows; they were not molested. American residents also posted signs on the doors of their homes.

The police and uniformed Storm Troopers are now patrolling the streets or are placed as sentries outside Jewish-owned shops and homes.

Making the Jews Pay for Kristallnacht

The cost of the broken glass alone came to 5 million marks, the equivalent of well over $2 million. Any compensation claims paid to Jews by insurance companies were confiscated by the Reich. The rubble of ruined synagogues had to be cleared by the Jewish community. Jews of German nationality, unlike Jewish-owned corporations from abroad, could not file for damages. A fine of one billion Reichmarks ($400 million) was imposed collectively on the Jewish community. After assessing the fine, [Nazi leader Hermann] Goering, who had assumed control in the aftermath from [Nazi propaganda minister Joseph] Goebbels, said: "I would not like to be a Jew in Germany." Harsher decrees followed immediately thereafter.

SOURCE. *Lionel Kochan and Michael Berenbaum, "Kristallnacht," Encyclopedia Judaica. Ed. Michael Berenbaum and Fred Skolnik. Vol. 12, 2nd ed. Detroit: Macmillan Reference USA, 2007.*

Jewish hospitals and schools were not attacked—among them is the well known Philantropen College, one of Europe's leading Jewish schools.

Reports from Other Towns

Wireless to *The New York Times*.

The wave of destruction of Jewish synagogues, homes, shops and other buildings in towns outside Berlin was reported as follows in the press today:

Eberswalde: Roof and interior of the synagogue in the Bismarckstrasse opposite ancient city walls destroyed by fire this morning.

Stettin: The Jewish temple opposite the Gruene Schanze (green bulwarks) was ablaze this morning. The fire brigade was unable to save any of the contents of the building and military pioneers were called to blast the ruins.

Landsberg: The synagogue's interior was ruined by fire in the early hours this morning.

Konstanz on the Bodensee: The synagogue was destroyed this morning.

Cologne: Jewish-owned shops were attacked and the Cologne synagogue was burned down last night.

Luebeck: Jewish-owned shops were demolished and synagogue windows smashed.

Leipzig: The windows of Jewish-owned shops were smashed and the Bamberger and Hertz Company, a department store, was set on fire as well as the synagogue.

Nuremberg: Jewish-owned shops were demolished.

Essen: In Essen and Duesseldorf the synagogues were reported blazing. A large Jewish youth home at Essen, just completed, was burned down.

Hamburg: Furious crowds demonstrated before Jewish-owned shops. Synagogues were attacked.

Potsdam: Jewish-owned shop windows were smashed and a synagogue on the Wilhelmplatz also suffered. Weapons were reported found in them.

Photo on previous page: German Jews—already the victims of vandalism and brutality on Kristallnacht, November 9, 1938—were forced to pay for the damage inflicted on their property. (**AP Photo.**)

Kottbus: A Jewish temple was set on fire.

Brandenburg: A Jewish temple was burned down.

The Nazis Isolate Jews in the Warsaw Ghetto in Poland

Mary Berg

During the Holocaust, only limited information reached the United States and its allies regarding the herding of Jews into "ghettos" in Germany and Poland. In these walled-off sections of cities, hundreds of thousands of Jews were forced to live in areas suitable for only a fraction of the number of residents. Food supplies were limited, and Nazi soldiers treated the ghetto residents with disdain and often brutalized them. In the following viewpoint, Mary Berg, a young Jewish resident of the Warsaw ghetto in Poland, writes about life there in the first months after its establishment. This excerpt from her larger diary was published in the United States in 1945 as World War II was just coming to an end, and it is one of the first firsthand accounts of life in the Warsaw ghetto published in English. Berg describes

SOURCE. Mary Berg, "Chapter II: The Ghetto Begins," *Warsaw Ghetto: A Diary by Mary Berg*. Edited by S.L. Shneiderman. OneWorld Publications, 1945, pp. 38–47; 49. Reproduced by permission.

not only the hardships but also the continuing normalcy that the ghetto residents attempted to create even in such cramped and often squalid conditions. Berg and her family—her mother was a US citizen—eventually made it to the United States when they were traded for German prisoners of war.

*N*ovember 15, 1940. Today the Jewish ghetto was officially established [in Warsaw, Poland]. Jews are forbidden to move outside the boundaries formed by certain streets. There is considerable commotion. Our people are hurrying about nervously in the streets, whispering various rumors, one more fantastic than the other.

Work on the walls—which will be three yards high—has already begun. Jewish masons, supervised by Nazi soldiers, are laying bricks upon bricks. Those who do not work fast enough are lashed by the overseers. It makes me think of the Biblical description of our slavery in Egypt. But where is the Moses who will release us from our new bondage?

At the end of those streets in which the traffic has not been stopped completely there are German sentries. Germans and Poles are allowed to enter the isolated quarter, but they must not carry any parcels. The specter of starvation looms up before us all.

Emptiness and Isolation in the Ghetto

November 20, 1940. The streets are empty. Extraordinary meetings are taking place in every house. The tension is terrific. Some people demand that a protest be organized. This is the voice of the youth; our elders consider this a dangerous idea. We are cut off from the world. There are no radios, no telephones, no newspapers. Only the hospitals and Polish police stations situated inside the ghetto are allowed to have telephones.

The Jews who have been living on the "Aryan" [the master race as defined by Adolf Hitler and the Nazis] side of the city were told to move out before November 12. Many waited until the last moment, because they hoped that the Germans, by means of protests or bribes, might be induced to countermand the decree establishing the ghetto. But as this did not come to pass many of our people were compelled to leave their beautifully furnished apartments at a moment's notice, and they arrived in the ghetto carrying only a few bundles in their hands.

Christian firms within the limits of the isolated Jewish quarter are allowed to remain temporarily if they have been there for at least twenty-five years. Many Polish and German factories are situated within the ghetto, and thanks to their employees we have a little contact with the outer world.

November 22, 1940. The ghetto has been isolated for a whole week. The red-brick walls at the end of the ghetto streets have grown considerably higher. Our miserable settlement hums like a beehive. In the homes and in the courtyards, wherever the ears of the Gestapo do not reach, people nervously discuss the Nazis' real aims in isolating the Jewish quarter. And how shall we get provisions? And who will maintain order? Perhaps it will really be better, perhaps we will be left in peace? . . .

> The official ration cards entitle one to a quarter of a pound of bread a day, one egg a month, and two pounds of vegetable jam (sweetened with saccharine) a month.

Food Becomes Scarce

December 15, 1940. . . . The question of obtaining food is becoming ever more pressing. The official ration cards entitle one to a quarter of a pound of bread a day, one egg a month, and two pounds of vegetable jam (sweetened with saccharine) a month. A pound of potatoes costs one zloty. We have forgotten even the taste of fresh fruit. Nothing can be imported from the "Aryan" districts although there is an abundance of everything there. But hunger and the desire for profit are stronger than all the penalties threatening smugglers, and smuggling is now gradually becoming an important industry.

Sienna Street, which forms one of the boundaries of the ghetto, is separated by walls only from the streets that cross it; the houses whose courtyards give on Zlota Street (Zlota is parallel to Sienna), the so-called "other side," are temporarily separated from the outer world by barbed wire. Most of the smuggling takes place here. Our windows give on such a courtyard. All night long there is a commotion there, and by morning carts with vegetables appear in the streets and the stores are filled with bread. There is even sugar, butter, cheese—of course for high prices, for people have risked their lives to get these things.

Sometimes a German sentry is bribed and a whole wagon full of all kinds of merchandise manages to get through the gates.

The Germans have demanded that the Jewish community administration take steps to stop the smuggling. They have also ordered that a Jewish militia be formed to help the Polish police in maintaining order in the ghetto. The community is trying to recruit two thousand able-bodied men between the ages of twenty-one and thirty-five. War veterans are given preference. A high educational standard is also required: a certificate from a gymnasium is the minimum.

Jewish Police Enforce Nazi Law

December 22, 1940. The Jewish police is an accomplished fact. More candidates presented themselves than were needed. A special committee chose them, and "pull" played an important part in their choice. At the very end, when only a few posts were available, money helped, too. . . . Even in Heaven not everyone is a saint.

Photo on following page: The Warsaw ghetto's Jewish police force was one example of how the Nazis set wartime Jews against one another. (Getty Images.)

The chief commissioner of this ghetto police is Colonel Szerynski, a converted Jew who was the police chief of Lublin before the war. Under him are three assistant commissioners: Hendel, Lejkin and Firstenberg, who together form the supreme police council. Then come the regional commandants, the district chiefs (the regions are divided into districts), and finally the ordinary policemen who perform routine duties.

> Meanwhile life is being organized in the ghetto. Work helps one to forget everything, and it is not hard to get work here.

Their uniform consists of a dark blue police cap and a military belt to which a rubber club is attached. Over the visor of the cap there is a metal badge bearing the Star of David and the inscription *Jüdischer Ordnungsdienst* (Jewish Order Service). On a blue ribbon around the cap, the policeman's rank is indicated by special signs: one round tin disk the size of a thumbnail for a policeman, two for a senior policeman, three for a district chief; one star for a regional commandant, two stars for the three assistant commissioners, and four for the commissioner himself.

Just like all the other Jews the Jewish policemen must wear a white arm band with the blue Star of David, but in addition they wear a yellow arm band with the inscription *Jüdischer Ordnungsdienst*. They also wear metallic badges with their numbers on their chests.

Among the duties of these new Jewish policemen are the following: guarding the gates of the ghetto together with German gendarmes and Polish policemen; directing traffic in the ghetto streets; guarding post offices, kitchens and the community administration; detecting and suppressing smugglers. The most difficult task of the Jewish police is the curbing of beggars—this actually consists in driving them from one street to another, because there is nothing else to do with them, especially as their number is growing from hour to hour. . . .

Suspicion of Jewish Officials Grows

December 25, 1940. Today a new group of uniformed Jewish officials appeared in the ghetto. They belong to the special Commission for the Fight Against Speculators, whose task it is to regulate the prices of various articles. For some time this organization has functioned in secret, but now it is out in the open. These officials wear the same kind of cap as the Jewish policemen, but with a green band, and instead of the policemen's yellow arm bands, they wear lavender arm bands with the inscription, "Fight Against Speculators."

While the attitude of the Jewish population toward the Jewish policemen is cordial, these new officials are treated with marked reserve because they are suspected of being tools of the Gestapo. Their organization has been nicknamed "The Thirteen," because its office is at 13 Leszno Street. Its chief is Commissar Szternfeld; his main collaborators are Gancwajch, Roland Szpunt and the lawyer Szajer of Lodz.

There is another group of uniformed Jewish officials in the ghetto—the workers of the ambulance unit, who wear a blue band on their caps, and blue arm bands. Still another is the black-clad corps of undertakers employed by private companies, among which the most popular are Pinkiert's, next to the community building on the Grzybowska, and Wittenberg's, directly across the street. Even to move into the next world is not very easy these days. Funerals are frightfully expensive, and a lot in the overcrowded Jewish cemetery is as precious as gold.

Meanwhile life is being organized in the ghetto. Work helps one to forget everything, and it is not hard to get work here. A great number of workshops and factories have opened; they make all sorts of articles that have never before been manufactured in Warsaw.

Our theatrical group has received several invitations to give performances in cafés. We also have our own hall, and intend to give regular shows two or three times a week in the afternoon. We have rented Weisman's dancing school on Panska Street, although it had an unsavory reputation before the war because the Warsaw underworld used to meet there. The inhabitants of the quarter once called this hall the "old joint." But now we have our own public, which will disregard the bad reputation of the hall and attend our shows no matter where they are given. Moreover there is no better hall in the whole so-called Little Ghetto that lies between Sienna and Leszno Streets.

The way from the Little Ghetto to the Big Ghetto begins at the corner of Chlodna and Zelazna Streets. Only the roadway, separated from the rest of Chlodna Street by walls on each side, is considered part of the ghetto. In the middle of the street there is an exit to Zelazna Street. This exit is especially well guarded by a Nazi gendarme armed with a machine gun, and two policemen, one Jewish and one Polish. . . .

Nazis Mistreat Jewish Policemen

January 4, 1941. The ghetto is covered with deep snow. The cold is terrible and none of the apartments are heated. Wherever I go I find people wrapped up in blankets or huddling under feather beds, that is, if the Germans have not yet taken all these warm things for their own soldiers. The bitter cold makes the Nazi beasts who stand guard near the ghetto entrances even more savage than usual. Just to warm up as they lurch back and forth in the deep snow, they open fire every so often and there are many victims among the passers-by. Other guards who are bored with their duty at the gates arrange entertainments for themselves. For instance, they choose a victim from among the people who chance to go by, order him to throw himself in the snow with his face down, and if he is a Jew who wears a beard, they tear it off together with the skin until the snow is red with blood. When such a Nazi is in a bad mood, his victim may be a Jewish policeman who stands guard with him.

Yesterday I myself saw a Nazi gendarme "exercise" a Jewish policeman near the passage from the Little to the Big Ghetto on Chlodna Street. The young man finally lost his breath, but the Nazi still forced him to fall and rise until he collapsed in a pool of blood. Then someone called for an ambulance, and the Jewish policeman was put on a stretcher and carried away on a hand truck. There are only three ambulance cars for the whole ghetto, and for that reason hand trucks are mostly used. We call them rikshas. . . .

Organizations Create a Sense of Unity

January 30, 1941. Today we held the inaugural meeting of the Youth Club of our block on Sienna Street. Similar clubs have been formed in all the streets of the ghetto. We have elected as president Manfred Rubin, an intelligent young German Jewish refugee, who came to Poland shortly before the war.

Engineer Stickgold greeted us in the name of the house committees of Sienna Street. He urged us to study as hard as possible and to share among ourselves not only our bread but also our knowledge. Every member of our group at once began to prepare a subject for a talk.

February 5, 1941. There is panic among the inhabitants of Sienna Street, for the rumor has spread that the street will be cut off from the ghetto, allegedly because of the extensive smuggling that is carried on here. But this is certainly not the real reason, for the same is true of all the border streets, and if one street is cut off, the smuggling will simply be transferred to the next one. The Germans themselves are circulating rumors that Sienna Street will be left to the Jewish inhabitants if they pay a contribution. This must be the real reason for the threat—the Germans want to get a large sum of money out of the inhabitants of the ghetto. . . .

February 15, 1941. One after another the ghetto streets have been shut off. Now only Poles are used for

> Now the walls are growing taller and taller and there are no loose bricks.

this work. The Nazis no longer trust the Jewish masons, who deliberately leave loose bricks in many places in order to smuggle food or to escape to the "other side" through the holes at night.

Now the walls are growing taller and taller and there are no loose bricks. The top is covered with a thick layer of clay strewn with glass splinters, intended to cut the hands of people who try to escape.

Ghetto Inhabitants Persevere

But the Jews still find ways. The sewer pipes have not been cut off, and through the openings they get in small bags of flour, sugar, cereal, and other articles. During dark nights they also take advantage of holes made in the gates to bring in foodstuffs. The removal of one brick is sufficient. Special packages are prepared to fit these holes.

There are other ways, too. Many bombed houses are situated on the border between the ghetto and the "other side." The cellars of these houses often form long tunnels that extend for three, four, or five houses. The greatest part of the smuggling is carried on through these tunnels. The Germans know this, but are unable to control the traffic.

Meanwhile the Nazis are cutting out of the ghetto the larger and more modern apartment houses. A number of streets have been split in two: one side belongs to the ghetto, the other to the "Aryan" side. In the middle of the street there is barbed wire or a wall. We tremble lest the same thing be done with Sienna Street, where we live, because the most beautiful houses in the whole quarter are on that street.

The Atrocities Committed at Concentration Camps

Gerhart Riegner

Gerhart Riegner was a member of the World Jewish Congress who, in 1942, alerted the Allied Powers to Adolf Hitler's plan to exterminate European Jewry. The following viewpoint is a report that Riegner passed on to US secretary of state Cordell Hull detailing information gleaned from escapees of concentration camps in Poland. The report describes the inhumane work conditions in Auschwitz (Oswieczim) and its sister camp Birkenau and the routine extermination of Jewish prisoners sent to these camps. The escapees speak of hard labor, little food, forced sterilizations, and rampant disease that killed off large numbers of the prison populations. More pressingly, though, they describe how many Jewish prisoners never suffered these brutal conditions because they were herded into gas chambers

---

SOURCE. Gerhart Riegner, "Summary of the Auschwitz Escapees Report, Sent under Cover of R.E. Shoenfeld, U.S. Charge to Czech Government in London, to Cordell Hull, Secretary of State, July 5, 1944," *The American Experience* (PBS), July 5, 1944. Reproduced by permission.

upon arrival and instantly killed. Riegner adds a few recommendations from the officials who smuggled the reports out of occupied Europe. They call upon the Allies to warn the Nazi government against continuing these murders and to immediately bomb the camp crematoria used to dispose of the bodies of the massacred Jews and the railway lines leading into the camps. The Allies, however, did not heed the advice.

The Czechoslovak Government has received through its representative in a neutral country an extract from the document drawn up regarding the fate of the Jews in the German camp at Birkenau. This document was drawn up at Bratislava by two Slovak Jews who had managed to escape from the camps at Oswieczim [Auschwitz] and Birkenau in April [1944]. It contains an urgent request for the Allies to be informed of the frightful conditions in these camps. The Czechoslovak Government considers it its duly to comply with this request and the following is a literal translation of the extract as received from the neutral country.

The information contained in the document has been further considerably supplemented by reports which a Polish major who escaped from Oswieczim furnished to the underground organization in Slovakia.

Physical Description of the Camps

The concentration camp at Oswieczim was originally intended for political prisoners, and about 15,000 Germans, Czechoslovaks, Poles and Russians were there in "protective detention". Besides this, professional criminals were sent there [as well as] homosexuals, Bible students, and later Jews from the occupied countries. Over the entrance is the inscription in German "Arbeit macht frei" ["Work brings freedom"].

The Birkenau labour camp, which lies 4 km. from Oswieczim, and the agricultural work of the Harmense camps are both under the control of the governor of the Oswieczim camp. Inside Oswieczim camp are workshops of the German armaments concerns Siemens and Krupp. The huts in the camp are in three rows covering an area of 500 x 300 metres. They are surrounded by a double fence 3 metres high charged with high tension electricity. At every 500 metres is a watch-tower 5 metres high with machine-guns and search-lights. This is the "kleine Postenkette" ["small cordon"]. Another line of watch-towers runs in a circle of 2 kilometres and the work-shops are between the two rows of watch-towers.

Birkenau camp is formed of three blocks covering an area 1,600 x 850 metres and is also surrounded by two rings of watch-towers. The outer ring is connected with the outer ring of watch-towers of Oswieczim camp and they are only separated by the railway-lines. Birkenau camp is called after the small forest of Birkenwald (in Polish Brzezinky) nearby. The local population used to call this place "Rajsko".

> Working conditions at Birkenau and Oswieczim [Auschwitz] are unimaginable.

Slave Labor and Institutionalized Murder

Working conditions at Birkenau and Oswieczim are unimaginable. Work is carried on either in the camp or in the neighbourhood. Roads are built. Reinforced concrete buildings are put up. Gravel is quarried. Houses in the neighbourhood are knocked down. New buildings are put up in the camps and in the work-shops. Work is also done in the neighbouring coal mines or in the factory for synthetic rubber. Some persons also work in the administration of the camps. Any person who does not carry out his work to the satisfaction of the overseer is flogged or beaten to death. The food is 300 grammes of bread per head every evening, or 1 litre per head of

Death typically proved to be the release promised to inmates by the slogan "work brings freedom" above the gates of Auschwitz. (AFP/Getty Images.)

turnip soup and a little coffee. That is for the Jews. Non-Jews receive rather more. Anyone who cannot work and has a temperature of at least 38.6 degrees is sent to the "Krankenbau", the hut for the sick. The German doctor divides sick persons into two groups: curable and seriously ill. The seriously ill are disposed of by a phenol injection in the region of the heart. Among non-Jews this is done only to those who are really seriously ill, while among the Jews 80 to 90 percent of all those ill receive it. 15,000 to 20,000 persons have already been got rid of in this way by injections. Particularly inhuman scenes took place when the sick were killed wholesale during the process of delousing when a typhus epidemic broke out. Near the "Krankenbau" is the "hygiene institute" where sterilisation and artificial insemination of the women are carried out and blood tests are made for blood transfusion. For these experiments chiefly Jews are used. Since March, 1942 enormous transports of Jews have come to Oswieczim and Birkenau. A very small number of them have been sent to the labor camp, while an average of 90 percent of those who have come have been taken straight from the train and killed. These executions took place at the beginning in the forest of Birkenwald by gas suffocation in a special building constructed for the purpose. After the suffocation by gas the dead bodies were burnt. At the end of February, 1943, four new crematoria were built, two large and two small, in the camp of Birkenau itself. The crematorium contains a large hall, a gas chamber and a furnace. People are assembled in the hall which holds 2,000 and gives the impression of a swimming-bath. They have to undress and are given a piece of soap and a towel as if they were going to the baths. Then they are crowded into the gas chamber which is hermetically sealed. Several S.S. men in gas-masks then pour into the gas chamber through three openings in the ceiling a preparation of the poison gas megacyklon, which is made in Hamburg [Germany]. At the end of three minutes all the persons are dead. The dead bodies are then taken away in carts to the furnace to be burnt. The furnace has nine chambers, each of them with four openings. Each opening will take three bodies at once. They are completely burnt after 1.5 hours. Thus each crematorium can burn 1,500 bodies daily. The crematoria can be recognized from outside by their lofty chimneys.

> A very small number of [Jews brought by train to Auschwitz and Birkenau] have been sent to the labor camp, while an average of 90 percent of those who have come have been taken straight from the train and killed.

Josef Mengele—"The Angel of Death"

Born 16 March 1911, [Josef] Mengele lived comfortably with his wealthy, devoutly Roman Catholic, Bavarian family. Choosing an academic career, he began his studies at the University of Munich in 1930, where he also embraced National Socialist ideology. The politics of the age apparently influenced Mengele's interests; he chose to study anthropology and medicine, interested in how genetic and other manipulations might improve a race. . . .

In May 1943 Mengele became a camp doctor at Auschwitz, hoping to use this assignment as a stepping-stone to an academic career. He executed his duties with a flourish that impressed colleagues and terrified inmates. Shortly after his arrival he quelled a typhus epidemic by sending hundreds of inmates to the gas chambers with no apparent regard for their lives. Among their duties, the doctors selected which inmates went immediately to the gas chambers and which inmates were assigned to labor details. Unlike most of the other SS [Nazi troop] doctors, Mengele appeared to relish this responsibility, performing selections more frequently than required.

In a laboratory located in Crematorium 2, outfitted with modern equipment and staffed by inmate professionals,

Hiding the Truth of Jewish Genocide

On principle only Jews are put to death by gas, this is only done to Aryans in exceptional cases. Aryans are shot with pistols on a special execution ground which lies between blocks 10 and 11 of Oswieczim camp. The first executions took place there in the summer of 1941 and reached their peak a year later when they were carried out by [the] hundreds. Later when this aroused attention a large number of non-Jews who were condemned to death were taken straight from the train to the execution ground and not entered on the lists of the camp. According to careful calculations during the period from April, 1942, to April, 1944, from 1.5 to 1.75 million Jews were put to death by gas or in some other way, half of these being Polish Jews, other Jews from Holland, Greece,

Mengele subjected prisoners to an array of injections and other caustic and toxic procedures in his quest to discover keys to the genetic manipulation of supposed Aryan features. Mengele particularly used twins, one serving as subject and the other the control. After the test, both twins might be fatally injected and immediately dissected to determine the impact of the test. Dyes were injected into eyes to see whether eye color could be altered. These tests, which had dubious scientific value, were conducted without any regard for the subjects themselves. Mengele also participated in the ongoing research on human sterilization, which was intended to find ways to prevent the reproduction of "undesirable" groups, thus guaranteeing the supposed racial purity of the Germans. Literally thousands of people suffered from the brutal treatments directed by Mengele; many perished.

SOURCE. *Larry Thornton, "Mengele, Josef (1911–1979),"* Europe Since 1914: Encyclopedia of the Age of War and Reconstruction. *Ed. John Merriman and Jay Winter. Vol. 3. Detroit: Charles Scribner's Sons, 2006.*

France, Belgium, Germany, Yugoslavia, Czechoslovakia, Italy, Norway, Lithuania, Austria and Jews of various other nationalities who were brought to Oswieczim from other camps in Poland. About 90 percent of the members of the transports arriving in Birkenau and Oswieczim were taken straight from the train to be put to death and about 10 percent became inmates of the camp.

Each of the new inmates was registered and received a number. In April, 1944, 180,000 persons in all had been registered as inmates of the camp, counting Jews and non-Jews together. Of the whole number who had arrived before there were only 34,000 in the camp at the beginning of April this year, 18,000 of them being non-Jews. (In both the sources that we have quoted this number includes the membership of both camps together.)

The remainder had been killed by hard work, illness, especially epidemics of typhus and malaria, ill treatment, and finally "selection". Twice a week the camp doctor indicated persons destined for selection. Those selected were all gassed. In a single block of Birkenau camp the average number of deaths a week was as much as 2,000, 1,200 of these being natural deaths and 800 "selection". A special book entitled "S.B. Sonderbehandelte" ["Special Treatment"] is kept dealing with the "selected". Notice of the deaths of the others is sent to the supreme commander of the camp at Oranienburg. At the beginning of 1943 the "political section" (camp Gestapo) at Oswieczim received 500,000 forms for release. The governor had them all made out in the names of persons who had already been gassed and lodged them in the archives of the camp. Among the persons responsible for the savagery in both camps we must mention:

> In a single block of Birkenau camp the average number of deaths a week was as much as 2,000.

[Rudolf] Hoess, governor of the camp, Untersturm-fuehrer Schwarzhuber, director of the camp, the Tyrolese chief of the political department (Lagerfuehrer), Ober-scharfuehrer, Palitsch, Scharfuehrer Stiwett, S.S. Schar-fuehrer Wykleff, S.S. Man Kler, the garrison doctor Wirt, the camp doctor Entrest. In addition, professional criminals who have killed Jews in the camp: Reich Germans Alexander Neumann, Albert Haemmerle, Rudi Osteringer, Rudi Berckert, Arno Boem, Eimmer and the political prisoners Alfred Kien and Aloid Stahler.

The Allies Must Take Action

The above is the contents of the two documents. The persons who have managed to secure the transmission of the documents to a neutral country added

(a) the following information:

MAJOR CONCENTRATION CAMPS AND DEATH CAMPS

★ Capital city

● Concentration camp

⊖ Death camp

Taken From: About.com.

"12,000 Jews are being deported daily from the territories of Carpathian Ruthenia, Transylvania and the district of Kosice where there used to be 320,000 Jews. Those departed are sent to Oswieczim, 5,000 going by train via Slovakia daily and 7,000 via Carpathian Ruthenia."

and (b) the following suggestions:

1. The Allied Governments, especially those whose citizens are suffering in both these camps, should jointly address to the Germans and Hungarians a threat of reprisals directed at the Germans in the hands of these governments.

> "The crematoria in both camps, which are recognisable by their high chimneys and watch-towers, should be bombed."

2. The crematoria in both camps, which are recognisable by their high chimneys and watch-towers, should be bombed and so should the main railway-lines connecting Slovakia and Carpathian Ruthenia with Poland which are also of military importance, (especially the bridge at Cop).

3. Public warnings to the Germans and Hungarians should be repeated.

4. The Vatican should be requested to pronounce a severe public condemnation.

The Nuremberg Trials Document the War Crimes of the Holocaust

Robert Jackson

A former US attorney general, Robert Jackson was a Supreme Court justice and the chief US prosecutor at the Nuremberg Trials, which sought to bring war criminals from World War II Axis powers—Germany, Italy, and Japan—to justice. The following viewpoint is an excerpt of Jackson's opening statement on November 21, 1945, to this international tribunal judging the fate of select Nazis accused of perpetrating crimes against humanity. In it, Jackson provides evidence from Nazi government records that details the harassment, forced confinement, and eventual slaughter of European Jews. He points to specific memorandums and other official letters to accuse the Nazi defendants of willful discrimination and of the murder of millions of Jews in Germany, Poland, and other countries under Nazi control. As a result of this evidence and other testimony from international prosecutors, several of the defendants—including Martin Bormann, Hans Frank, Wilhelm Frick, Alfred Rosenberg, and Arthur Seyss-Inquart—were condemned to death.

SOURCE. Courtesy of Government Printing Office.

The privilege of opening the first trial in history for crimes against the peace of the world imposes a grave responsibility. The wrongs which we seek to condemn and punish have been so calculated, so malignant and so devastating, that civilization cannot tolerate their being ignored because it cannot survive their being repeated. That four great nations, flushed with victory and stung with injury, stay the hand of vengeance and voluntarily submit their captive enemies to the judgment of the law is one of the most significant tributes that Power ever has paid to Reason.

This tribunal, while it is novel and experimental, is not the product of abstract speculations nor is it created to vindicate legalistic theories. This inquest represents the practical effort of four of the most mighty of nations, with the support of seventeen more, to utilize International Law to meet the greatest menace of our times—aggressive war. The common sense of mankind demands that law shall not stop with the punishment of petty crimes by little people. It must also reach men who possess themselves of great power and make deliberate and concerted use of it to set in motion evils which leave no home in the world untouched. It is a cause of this magnitude that the United Nations will lay before Your Honors.

> What makes this inquest significant is that those prisoners represent sinister influence that will lurk in the world long after their bodies have returned to dust.

The Faces of Evil

In the prisoners' dock sit twenty-odd broken men. Reproached by the humiliation of those they have led almost as bitterly as by the desolation of those they have attacked, their personal capacity for evil is forever past. It is hard now to perceive in these miserable men as captives the power by which as Nazi leaders they once dominated much of the world and terrified most of it. Merely as individuals, their fate is of little consequence to the world.

What makes this inquest significant is that those prisoners represent sinister influence that will lurk in the world long after their bodies have returned to dust. They are living symbols of racial hatreds, of terrorism and violence, and of the arrogance and cruelty of power. They are symbols of fierce nationalisms and militarism, of intrigue and war-making which have embroiled Europe generation after generation, crushing its manhood, destroying its homes, and impoverishing its life. They have so identified themselves with the philosophies they conceived and with the forces they directed that any tenderness to them is a victory and an encouragement to all the evils which are attached to their names. Civilization can afford no compromise with the social forces which would gain renewed strength if we deal ambiguously or indecisively with the men in whom those forces now precariously survive.

What these men stand for we will patiently and temperately disclose. We will give you undeniable proofs of incredible events. The catalogue of crimes will omit nothing that could be conceived by a pathological pride, cruelty, and lust for power. These men created in Germany, under the *Fuehrerprinzip* [political leadership resting on a single person], a National Socialist despotism equalled only by the dynasties of the ancient East. They took from the German people all those dignities and freedoms that we hold natural and inalienable rights in every human being. The people were compensated by inflaming and gratifying hatreds toward those who were marked as "scapegoats." Against their opponents, includ-

> When the Nazi Party gained control of the German State, the conspirators used the means of official decrees as a weapon against the Jews.

ing Jews, Catholics, and free labor, the Nazis directed such a campaign of arrogance, brutality, and annihilation as the world has not witnessed since the pre-Christian ages. They excited the German ambition to be a "master race," which of course implies serfdom for others. They led their people on a mad gamble for domination. They diverted social energies and resources to the creation of what they thought to be an invincible war machine. They overran their neighbors. To sustain the "master race" in its war making, they enslaved millions of human beings and brought them into Germany, where these hapless creatures now wander as "displaced persons." At length bestiality and bad faith reached such excess that they aroused the sleeping strength of imperiled civilization. Its united efforts have ground the German war machine to fragments. But the struggle has left Europe a liberated yet prostrate land where a demoralized society struggles to survive. These are the fruits of the sinister forces that sit with these defendants in the prisoners' dock. . . .

Discrimination Against the Jews

When the Nazi Party gained control of the German State, the conspirators used the means of official decrees as a weapon against the Jews. In this way the force of the state was applied against them.

Jewish immigrants were denaturalized (1933 *Reichsgesetzblatt* [*Reiche Law Gazette*], signed by [Minister of the Interior Wilhelm] Frick and [former Minister of Foreign Affairs Baron Konstantin von] Neurath).

Native Jews were precluded from citizenship (1935, signed by Frick).

Jews were forbidden to live in marriage or to have extra-marital relations with persons of German blood (1935, signed by Frick and [Nazi architect Rudolf] Hess).

Jews were denied the right to vote (1936, signed by Frick).

Photo on following page: Leaders of Nazi Germany (seated) faced international justice in the 1945–1946 Nuremberg war crime trials. **(Getty Images.)**

Jews were denied the right to hold public office or civil service positions (1933, signed by Frick).

Jews were relegated to an inferior status by the denial of common privileges and freedoms. Thus, they were denied access to certain city areas, sidewalks, transportation, places of amusement, restaurants (1938). . . .

The Jews were also forced to pay discriminatory taxes and huge atonement fines. Their homes, bank accounts, real estate, and intangibles were expropriated. . . .

Finally, in 1943, the Jews were placed beyond the protection of any judicial process by a decree signed by [Nazi Party secretary Martin] Bormann and Frick, among others; the police were made the sole arbiters of punishment and death (1943, signed by Frick and Bormann). . . .

Registration and Segregation of Jews in German Occupied Territory

At this point the gradual and mounting campaign against the Jews was prepared for the achievement of its ultimate violent ends. The German people had been indoctrinated, and the seeds of hatred had been sown. The German state was armed and prepared for conquest. The force of world opinion could now safely be ignored. Already the Nazi conspirators had forced out of Germany 200,000 of its former 500,000 Jews. The Nazi-controlled German state was therefore emboldened, and [leader Adolf] Hitler in anticipation of the aggressive wars already planned cast about for a provocation.

In his speech before the Reichstag [German parliament] on 30 January 1939, Hitler declared:

> If the international Jewish financiers within and without Europe succeed in plunging the nations once more into a world war, the result will not be the Botshevization of the world and the victory of Jewry, but the obliteration of the Jewish race in Europe. . . .

The first step in accomplishing the purpose of the Nazi Party and the Nazi-dominated state, to eliminate the Jew, was to require a complete registration of all Jews. Inasmuch as the anti-Jewish policy was linked with the program of German aggression, such registration was required not only within the Reich, but successively within the conquered territories. For example, registration was required, by decree, within Germany (1938, signed by Frick); within Austria (1940); within Poland (*Kurjer Krakowski*, 24 October, 1939); in France (*Journal Official*, 30 September, 1940); in Holland (*Verordnungsblatt*, 10 January, 1941, signed by [Minister of Armaments Arthur] Seyss-Inquart).

> The Jews, having been registered and confined within the ghettos, now furnished a reservoir for slave labor.

The second step was to segregate and concentrate the Jews within restricted areas, called ghettos. This policy was carefully worked out, as is illustrated by the confidential statement taken from the files of [Minister of the Eastern Occupied Territories Alfred] Rosenberg. This memorandum of Rosenberg's, entitled "Directions for Handling of the Jewish Question," states:

> The first main goal of the German measures must be strict segregation of Jewry from the rest of the population. In the execution of this, first of all, is the seizing of the Jewish population by the introduction of a registration order and similar appropriate measures. . . .

Conditions within this ghetto are indicated in the statement of the report that an average of six persons lived in every room.

[SS (Nazi troops) chief Heinrich] Himmler [not present at the trials] received a report from the SS Brigade Fuehrer Group A, dated 15 October 1941, which further illustrates the establishment and operation of the ghettos. The report states: . . .

In Riga [Latvia] the so-called "*Moskau Suburb*" was designated as a ghetto. This is the worst dwelling district of Riga, already now mostly inhabited by Jews. The transfer of the Jews into the ghetto district proved rather difficult because the Latvians dwelling in that district had to be evacuated and residential space in Riga is very crowded. 24,000 of the 28,000 Jews living in Riga have been transferred into the ghetto so far. In creating the ghetto, the Security Police restricted themselves to mere policing duties, while the establishment and administration of the ghetto as well as the regulation of the food supply for the inmates of the ghetto were left to civil administration; the labor officers were left in charge of Jewish labor.

In the other towns with a larger Jewish population ghettos shall be established likewise. . . .

Using Jews as Forced Labor

The Jews, having been registered and confined within the ghettos, now furnished a reservoir for slave labor. The difference between slave labor and "labor duty" was this: the latter group were entitled to reasonable compensation, stated working hours, medical care and attention, and other social security measures, while the former were granted none of these advantages, being in fact, on a level below that of slaves.

Rosenberg set up within his organization for the Occupied Eastern Territories a department which, among other things, was to seek a solution for the Jewish problem by means of forced labor. . . .

Rosenberg issued instructions that Jewish forced labor should be utilized for every manual labor task:

The standing rule for the Jewish labor employment is the complete and unyielding use of Jewish manpower regardless of age in the reconstruction of the occupied eastern territories. . . .

Violations against German measures, especially

against the forced labor regulations, are to be punished by death to the Jews. . . .

The Concentration Camps and Death Camps Kill Millions

The concentration camps were utilized to dispose of literally millions of Jews, who died by mass shooting, gas, poison, starvation, and other means. The part which the concentration camps played in the annihilation of the Jewish people is indicated in an official Polish report on Auschwitz Concentration Camp. In Auschwitz during July 1944 Jews were killed at the rate of 12,000 daily:

> The concentration camps were utilized to dispose of literally millions of Jews, who died by mass shooting, gas, poison, starvation, and other means.

> During July 1944, they were being liquidated at the rate of 12,000 Hungarian Jews daily, and as the crematory could not deal with such numbers, many bodies were thrown into large pits and covered with quick lime.

The official Polish Government Commission Report on the Investigation of German Crimes in Poland describes the concentration camp at Treblinka in these terms:

> In March 1942, the Germans began to erect another camp, Treblinka B, in the neighborhood of Treblinka A, intended to become a place of torment for Jews.
>
> The erection of this camp was closely connected with the German plans aiming at a complete destruction of the Jewish population in Poland which necessitated the creation of a machinery by means of which the Polish Jews could be killed in large numbers. Late in April 1942, the erection of the first three chambers was finished in which these general massacres were to be performed by means of steam. Somewhat later the

erection of the real death building was finished, which contains ten death chambers. It was opened for wholesale murders early in autumn 1942.

The report of the Polish commission describes graphically the procedure for extermination within the camp:

The average number of Jews dealt with at the camp in summer 1942 was about two railway transports daily, but there were days of much higher efficiency. From autumn 1942 this number was falling.

After unloading in the siding all victims were assembled in one place where men were separated from women and children. In the first days of the existence of the camp the victims were made to believe that after a short stay in the camp, necessary for bathing and disinfection, they would be sent farther east, for work. Explanations of this sort were given by SS men who assisted at the unloading of the transports and further explanations could be read in notices stuck up on the walls of the barracks. But later, when more transports had to be dealt with, the Germans dropped all pretenses and only tried to accelerate the procedure.

All victims had to strip off their clothes and shoes, which were collected afterwards, whereupon all victims, women and children first, were driven into the death chambers. Those too slow or too weak to move quickly were driven on by rifle butts, by whipping and kicking. . . . Many slipped and fell, [and] the next victims pressed forward and stumbled over them. Small children were simply thrown inside. After being filled up to capacity the chambers were hermetically closed and steam was let in. In a few minutes all was over. The Jewish menial workers had to remove the bodies from the platform and to bury them in mass graves. By and by, as new transports arrived, the cemetery grew, extending in eastern direction.

From reports received, it may be assumed that several hundred thousands of Jews have been exterminated in Treblinka.

An official United States government report issued by the Executive Office of the President of the United States, War Refugee Board, on the German camps at Auschwitz and Birkenau, sets forth the number of Jews gassed in Birkenau in the two-year period between April 1942 and April 1944. The figure printed in this report is not a typographical error. The number is 1,765,000.

> "The huge scale of the Jewish eliminations is also reflected in the bookkeeping and statistics of the Germans themselves."

The huge scale of the Jewish eliminations is also reflected in the bookkeeping and statistics of the Germans themselves. The 16 December 1941 entry in the diary of [governor-general of occupied Poland] Hans Frank contains these figures:

> The Jews for us also represent extraordinarily malignant gluttons.
>
> We have now approximately 2,500,000 of them in General Government—perhaps with the Jewish mixtures, and everything that goes with it, 3,500,000 Jews.

On 25 January 1944, three years and one month later, Frank wrote in his diary these words:

> At the present time we still have in the General Government perhaps 100,000 Jews.

Thus, in this period of three years, according to the records of the then Governor General of Occupied Poland, between 2,400,000 and 3,400,000 Jews had been eliminated.

The total number of Jews who died by Nazi hands can never be definitely ascertained. It is known, however, that 4 million Jews died in concentration camps, and that 2 million Jews were killed by the State Police in the East, making a total of 6 million murdered Jews. The source of these figures is Adolph Eichmann, Chief of the Jewish Section of the Gestapo [secret police].

Jewish Germans Return to Their Hometown after the Holocaust Ends

Ernest O. Hauser

In the following viewpoint, Ernest O. Hauser, a columnist for the *Saturday Evening Post* and other periodicals, describes the repatriation of German Jews after World War II. He focuses on the city of Frankfurt, Germany, a community that deported or executed twenty thousand of its estimated twenty-eight thousand Jewish residents before and during the war. Hauser offers testimony from several Jews who escaped death and eventually returned to the city to pick up their lives and start over. According to Hauser, many Jews who came back faced German gentiles, who responded with a gamut of emotions from regret to continued hostility. However, according to Hauser's interviewees, Frankfurt was their home and these displaced Jews felt a kinship to the community they had left behind. Some of the returnees hoped the tragedy of the Holocaust could be forgotten

SOURCE. Ernest O. Hauser, "What's Happening to Germany's Jews?" *Saturday Evening Post*, September 17, 1949, pp. 19–21. Reproduced by permission.

so that a new Germany could emerge; others came back with a conviction that Germany owed them retribution for the hardships they had endured.

"Here," says the German and English inscription on a black marble plaque, "stood the Börne Platz Synagogue, which was destroyed by Nazi criminals on the 9th day of November, 1938." You look around for charred remnants of Frankfort's main synagogue, bits of masonry, perhaps, but there's nothing except the clean-swept square, flat as a tennis court. It takes someone familiar with the terrain to trace the still-distinguishable lines, a little darker than the rest of the ground, which show where the building once stood. That's all—annihilation was thorough.

That slab of black marble might well be the tombstone of Frankfort's once-great Jewish community. When [Nazi leader Adolf] Hitler came to power [in 1933], 28,000 Jews living in this city formed one of the largest, proudest, wealthiest and most historic Jewish communities in the Western world. Only 147 of them were left when the Americans took Frankfort twelve years later.

> Emerging from the gore and stench of history's greatest massacre, [Germany's Jews] are free to show their faces once again.

A few hundred more have come trudging back since then—a small, tattered band of people dwelling precariously among their enemies of yesterday. They are inconspicuous. The little woman in the big straw hat, selling imitation jewelry behind a rickety stand on the corner of the park; the man in the editorial office of a large daily newspaper; the young apprentice in the bakery; the fellow who runs the translation bureau—they're scattered here and there in the sprawling, ruined city.

Emerging from the gore and stench of history's greatest massacre, they are free to show their faces once again. But all of them have lost close relatives—some are the sole survivors of thriving, closely knit families of as many as fifty members. Sitting here, among the ruins of their past and the ghosts of their murdered relatives, what do these men and women think? What are their problems, their hopes? Why did they come back? The answer to this last question, sometimes, is pathetically simple: "I'm tired of running. I'm sick of strange surroundings. I was longing for home." And some will add, with shaky defiance, "My ancestors have lived in Frankfort for centuries; this is where I belong."

It's true, many of them are oldsters—and, as one of them said, "You can't transplant an old tree." Of Frankfort's Jewish community of 847 souls—not counting some 900 displaced Jews from Eastern Europe still waiting here for their turn to move on—more than one third are fifty-five years of age and over. Most of the young ones talk of leaving someday, and their elders would like to see them go. There's little enthusiasm over the fact that the German authorities are rebuilding, at state expense, one of Frankfort's main synagogues, burned down by the Nazis. "What for? There'll never be enough Jews here to fill it." Each Jew, pitching his

> Talk with some of the returned Jews, listen to their problems, fears and hopes, and you'll get as wide a variety of personal opinions and individual fates as there are people.

tent again among the Germans, is constantly searching his soul: "Whenever I pass a stranger on the street, how can I tell his hands aren't sullied with the blood of my brothers and sisters?" And, assuming they're not, "How can we establish the right relationship? It will take a brand-new set of attitudes on the part of the German people—a new respect for humanity—to make it possible for a Jew to feel at home again in Germany."

Talk with some of the returned Jews, listen to their problems, fears and hopes, and you'll get as wide a variety of personal opinions and individual fates as there are people. The composite picture is one of woeful confusion.

Old Feelings and Hatreds Persist

Meet the woman in the straw hat. She's Frau Binheim, one of the lucky ones—both her husband and little boy are alive. "They gave us a few years' grace because Hugo was wounded in the first World War. We weren't carted off by the Nazis till 1942. And the Americans brought us back when the war was over." Three short sentences covering a thousand miles of misery—beatings, deprivations, fiendish humiliations, forced labor, for both husband and wife; the annihilation of their entire families; the squalor and bleak despair of the walled ghetto of Theresienstadt, Czechoslovakia; and the void which is their world today.

"The Germans are polite," Frau Binheim says, "but they don't like us any better than before. Just the other day I was thinking of getting a larger stand, so I could have a better display, and one of the other street venders said, 'You people getting uppity again, eh?' It's a hostile world, and I often say to Hugo, 'Let's pack up and leave for good.' But without money, and without relatives abroad, it's too much of a jump. We'll stay, I guess."

Hugo, her husband, is in the patent-medicine business. He's to be seen at county fairs all over the country, lecturing on the advantages of his nose drops—a hard, meager business. Their little boy, blond, blue-eyed and, in the words of his mother, "too young to know whether he'll like it here," is in school; the other kids are friendly, as a rule—if they hit him or call him "Jew," which Frau Binheim estimates doesn't happen more than once every six weeks, they always draw a sharp reprimand from the teacher. The Binheims have a small apartment, and one

of the decorations, hung up on the parlor wall, is the yellow Star of David each Jew was forced to wear in Hitler's [Third] Reich—a sad relic of survival.

While few Jews are downright optimistic, there's a fairly widespread tendency to "give the Germans one more chance." "I think they can be cured of their deep-seated anti-Semitism," says forty-year-old Alfred Weber. "In fact, the word should never be mentioned—or the word 'Jew,' at that. Let the whole business be forgotten."

Weber, a short, sharp-faced, highly strung fellow who wears mustache and sideburns and has a penchant for

The yellow star that Nazis forced Jews to wear became, for some, "a sad relic of survival." **(Associated Press.)**

gay neckties, once owned a thriving motorcycle business. When Hitler came to power, he left Frankfort, where his ancestors have lived for the last 400 years, and became an interpreter at a travel agency in Paris. Hitler caught up with him and put him into a camp, but Alfred, deciding this wasn't for him, escaped to join the Maquis [French Resistance]—two bullet scars remain as souvenirs. Back in Frankfort with the Jewish girl he met and married in France and five boisterous offspring, he views the world around him without rancor. "As an old Frankfort citizen, I've got many friends here and they were glad to see me when I came back. Most of them are gentiles, but none of them were Nazis, I'm sure. We go to their homes, and they come here for dinner, and if we talk politics, it's the next war we talk about, not the last."

Rather than go back to the motorcycle business, for which he sees no immediate future in Germany, Weber plans to open a café in a bombed-out house now under repair. It will be called "Freddy's," and advertised as the first Jewish-owned café in postwar Frankfort. "I tell you, a Jew has a chance in this town," he says, beaming with confidence. Suddenly, his mood changes, "If anything happens here, I can always sell out and take my family to Israel." . . .

> [Jewish returnee] Harry [Hamburger] believes in slugging it out with the Germans, and takes no nonsense from them.

No Longer Submissive

"I think I can handle those Germans," says forty-six-year-old Harry Hamburger, a stocky, two-fisted realist who played a successful game of hide-and-seek with Hitler throughout the war. Formerly in the silk business, Harry now runs a translation bureau in a busy hotel near the railroad station. The handful of languages he picked up in exile nets dividends; things are humming in his little hotel-room office. "If all goes well, I'm here to stay."

Returning to his native Frankfort after an odyssey which took him in and out of Italy, France, Holland and Belgium, Harry was none the worse for wear, except that his marriage to a gentile had broken under the strain. "I swore that, if I ever married again, it would be a Jewish girl who'd been in concentration camp. I found one—at a tea dance here in Frankfort." Frau Hamburger, a pretty brunette, is a survivor of the Ravensbrück camp for women. When the Russians drew near in 1945, she and other prisoners were taken out and herded through the forest by Nazi women guards with police dogs, destination unknown. Just before the Russians appeared on the scene, the guards faded into the woods, but the emaciated Jewish women walked up to their liberators—who raped them.

Harry believes in slugging it out with the Germans, and takes no nonsense from them. Every week end, he goes fishing in a stream that comes rushing down from the Odenwald hills, making his headquarters in a small village nearby. There, one evening, two boys sneaked up behind him, yelled "Jew" and ran, but Harry gave chase on a hurriedly requisitioned bicycle. He caught them. "I could have spanked those kids myself, but, on second thought, turned them over to the schoolmaster, who did a really professional job."

Harry makes a point, too, of using the pink pass identifying him as a victim of Nazism, which gives him the right to go to the head of the queue whenever there is one. Most Jews, careful not to appear "pushy," prefer taking their place in line, but not Harry.

Only once was he bested. Unable to subscribe for his favorite newspaper because of the paper shortage, he went to see the circulation manager to complain. "How come all the Nazis in my apartment house are getting your paper every morning?"

"If they're Nazis," said the man, "they need it more than you. They have to be enlightened."

Back from Exile

A case apart is that of Alvin Rosengarten—the Jew who came back from Palestine. "My wife and I just couldn't stand the climate," he explains. "Besides, this is where we belong. We are Western Europeans, after all, and it was only natural for us to return to the kind of civilization in which we were born and raised." Now and then, of an evening, when they browse through the collection of photographs they brought back with them, the Rosengartens still shudder—"That hot blue sky, day after day . . . never a cloud . . . it drives you out of your mind."

Arrested and released seven times after Hitler came to power, Rosengarten left Frankfort, where he owned a prosperous travel bureau, in 1933. After knocking around Europe for six years, he finally went to Palestine. There he took a desk job with the British police and held it through the war, eking out the low pay by playing the piano in a Haifa café at night. When the British quit the mandate, Rosengarten, who had never driven roots into the foreign soil, bethought himself of his Frankfort travel bureau. He arrived here, with his wife and five children, just fourteen years after his departure.

How's business? Better than ever. From his newly built office on Frankfort's main drag, Alvin—a strapping fellow with a smiling, sunburned face—organizes low-cost mass excursions to the Bavarian Alps, chartering special trains to satisfy postwar Germany's travel-hungry public. He or his wife usually goes along with the groups of tourists to see that everything is all right.

"There's never any trouble," Frau Rosengarten says. "Once in a while, when a customer finds he's got no running water in his room, he'll mutter something about 'this Jewish-run business.' Let them talk."

But while Rosengarten is willing to trust the Germans as far as he and his wife are concerned, he hopes that his five children, four of whom were born in exile, will eventually move on. Rolf, the eldest, nearly sixteen, is now serving his apprenticeship in a Frankfort bakery. "The baker's trade," says Alvin, "is something international. Rolf will be able to make his living anywhere in the world—even in America."

A New Start

But the successful ones, the Rosengartens and Hamburgers, are few and far between; indeed, it's only a minority who have been able to get a bit of firm ground under their feet. An unhealthily large number still depend for their livelihood on the Jewish Religious Community—a once-wealthy organization incorporated under pre-Hitler German law, and now carrying on modestly in what used to be a Jewish kindergarten. Receiving occasional, carefully measured advances upon its ultimate damage claims from the German authorities, the corporation has taken it upon itself to provide work and homes for jobless, homeless Jews. More than 100 still live in the community-owned, half-ruined Jewish Hospital; and many are doing odd jobs around the Jewish cemetery and the Jewish relief kitchen here. It's nothing very solid, nothing very permanent, but it's just the thing for people with empty pockets and empty minds, lacking the initiative and confidence indispensable for a new start in life—just the thing for people bereft of yesterday and unsure of tomorrow.

> The successful [returning Jews] . . . are few and far between; indeed, it's only a minority who have been able to get a bit of firm ground under their feet.

CHAPTER 2

Controversies Concerning the Holocaust

The US Government Willfully Failed to Help European Jews Escape the Nazis

Josiah E. DuBois

After the United States officially entered World War II on December 8, 1941, the nation's fighting forces were committed primarily to the Pacific to stem the Japanese advance. It wasn't until 1943 that US troops set foot in Europe. While American soldiers were busy striking for the heart of Germany in 1943 and 1944, some critics accused the US government of failing to address the plight of the Jews in Europe in its grand strategy of liberation. In 1944, Josiah E. DuBois, a US Treasury official, issued a report to the Treasury secretary, Henry Morgenthau, Jr., that accused the US government of deliberately ignoring the European Jews and attempting to limit the public's knowledge of the atrocities being committed in the concentration camps.

Photo on previous page: Controversies involving the Holocaust include whether it should, or even can be, depicted in art or literature, and, for some, whether it happened at all. (**Associated Press.**)

SOURCE. Josiah E. DuBois, "Report to the Secretary on the Acquiescence of this Government in the Murder of the Jews," PBS, January 13, 1944. Reproduced by permission.

DuBois provides extensively detailed accounts of both how and when information about the Holocaust first reached the US government, as well as the limited response of the government to intervene and disrupt the ongoing murder of Jews. Morgenthau showed the document to US president Franklin D. Roosevelt, who maintained his position that the quickest way to save the Jews was to win the war.

One of the greatest crimes in history, the slaughter of the Jewish people in Europe, is continuing unabated.

This Government has for a long time maintained that its policy is to work out programs to serve those Jews of Europe who could be saved.

I am convinced on the basis of the information which is available to me that certain officials in our State Department, which is charged with carrying out this policy, have been guilty not only of gross procrastination and willful failure to act, but even of willful attempts to prevent action from being taken to rescue Jews from [Nazi leader Adolf] Hitler.

I fully recognize the graveness of this statement and I make it only after having most carefully weighed the shocking facts which have come to my attention during the last several months [in late 1943].

Unless remedial steps of a drastic nature are taken, and taken immediately, I am certain that no effective action will be taken by this Government to prevent the complete extermination of the Jews in German controlled Europe, and that this Government will have to share for all time responsibility for this extermination.

> Unless remedial steps of a drastic nature are taken, and taken immediately, I am certain that no effective action will be taken by this Government to prevent the complete extermination of the Jews in German controlled Europe.

The Multiple Failures of the US Government

The tragic history of the Government's handling of this matter reveals that certain State Department officials are guilty of the following:

They have not only failed to use the Governmental machinery at their disposal to rescue Jews from Hitler, but have even gone so far as to use this Government machinery to prevent the rescue of these Jews. . . .

They not only have failed to facilitate the obtaining of information concerning Hitler's plans to exterminate the Jews of Europe but in their official capacity have gone so far as to surreptitiously attempt to stop the obtaining of information concerning the murder of the Jewish population of Europe. . . .

Evidence of US Government Procrastination

The public record, let alone the facts which have not as yet been made pubic, reveals the gross procrastination and willful failure to act of those officials actively representing this Government in this field.

A long time has passed since it became clear that Hitler was determined to carry out a policy of exterminating the Jews in Europe.

Over a year has elapsed since this Government and other members of the United Nations publicly acknowledged and denounced this policy of extermination; and since the President gave assurances that the United States would make every effort together with the United Nations to save those who could be saved.

Despite the fact that time is most precious in this matter, State Department officials have been kicking the matter around for over a year without producing results; giving all sorts of excuses for delays upon delays; advancing no specific proposals designed to rescue Jews, at the same time proposing that the whole refugee problem be "explored" by this Government and Intergovernmental Committees. While the State Department has been thus "exploring" the whole refugee problem, without distinguishing between those who are in imminent danger of death and those who are not, hundreds of thousands of Jews have been allowed to perish.

Early Messages Warning of Hitler's Plans

As early as August 1942 a message from the Secretary of the World Jewish Congress in Switzerland, transmitted through the British Foreign Office, reported that Hitler had under consideration a plan to exterminate all Jews in German controlled Europe. By November 1942 sufficient evidence had been received, including substantial documentary evidence transmitted through our Legation in Switzerland, to confirm that Hitler had actually adopted and was carrying out his plan to exterminate the Jews. [American Foreign Service diplomat] Sumner Welles accordingly authorized the Jewish organizations to make the facts public.

Thereupon, the Jewish organizations took the necessary steps to bring the shocking facts to the attention of the public through mass meetings, etc. and to elicit public support for governmental action. On December 17, 1942, a joint statement of the United States and the European members of the United Nations was issued calling attention to and denouncing the fact that Hitler was carrying into effect his oft-repeated intention to exterminate the Jewish people in Europe.

Since the time when this Government knew that the Jews were being murdered, our State Department has failed to take any positive steps reasonably calculated to save any of these people. Although [the Department of] State has used the device of setting up intergovernmental organizations to survey the whole refugee problem, and calling conferences such as the Bermuda Conference

Photo on following page: European refugees aboard the MS *St. Louis* were among many who fled Nazi persecution but were turned away by the United States and other nations. (**Associated Press.**)

[between the United States and the United Kingdom] to explore the whole refugee problem, making it appear that positive action could be expected, in fact nothing has been accomplished.

Politicians Denounce US Inaction

Before the outcome of the Bermuda conference, which was held in April 1943, was made public, Senator [William] Langer prophetically stated in an address in the Senate on October 6, 1943:

> 'One of the most tragic factors about the situation is that . . . [the Jews] seem to have been forgotten by the nations which claim to fight for the cause of humanity.'

As yet we have had no report from the Bermuda Refugee Conference. With the best good will in the world and with all latitude that could and should be accorded to diplomatic negotiations in time of war, I may be permitted to voice the bitter suspicion that the absence of a report indicates only one thing—the lack of action.

Probably in all 5703 years, Jews have hardly had a time as tragic and hopeless as the one which they are undergoing now. One of the most tragic factors about the situation is that while singled out for suffering and martyrdom by their enemies, they seem to have been forgotten by the nations which claim to fight for the cause of humanity. *We* should remember the Jewish slaughterhouse of Europe and ask what is being done—and I emphasize the word "done"—to get some of these suffering human beings out of the slaughter while yet alive. . . .

Perhaps it would be necessary to introduce a formal resolution or to ask the Secretary of State to report to an appropriate congressional committee on the steps being taken in this connection. Normally it would have been the job of the Government to show itself alert to this tragedy; but when a government neglects a duty it is the job of the legislature in a democracy to remind it of that duty. . . . It is not important who voices a call for action, and it is not important what procedure is being used in order to get action. It is important that action be undertaken. . . .

The United States Limits the Number of Jewish Refugees

The most glaring example of the use of the machinery of this Government to actually prevent the rescue of Jews is the administrative restrictions which have been placed upon the granting of visas to the United States. In the note which the State Department sent to the British on February 25, 1943, it was stated:

> Since the entry of the United States into the war there have been no new restrictions placed by the Government of the United States upon the number of aliens of any nationality permitted to proceed to this country under existing laws, except for the more intensive examination of aliens required for security reasons.

The exception "for security reasons" mentioned in this note is the joker. Under the pretext of security reasons so many difficulties have been placed in the way of refugees obtaining visas that it is no wonder that the admission of refugees to this country does not come anywhere near the quota, despite [Assistant Secretary of State Breckinridge] Long's statement designed to create the impression to the contrary. The following administrative restrictions which have been applied to the issuance of visas since the beginning of the war are typical.

- Many applications for visas have been denied on the grounds that the applications have close relatives in Axis controlled Europe. The theory of this is that the enemy would be able to put pressure on the applicant as a result of the fact that the enemy has the power of life or death over his immediate family.

- Another restriction greatly increases the red tape and delay involved in getting the visa and requires among other things two affidavits of support and sponsorship to be furnished with each application for a visa. To each affidavit of support and sponsorship there must be attached two letters of reference from two reputable American citizens.

> Even if we took these [Jewish] refugees and treated them as prisoners of war it would be better than letting them die.

If anyone were to attempt to work out a set of restrictions specifically designed to prevent Jewish refugees from entering this country it is difficult to conceive of how more effective restrictions could have been imposed than have already been imposed on grounds of "security."

Alternative Means of Ensuring Security

It is obvious of course that these restrictions are not essential for security reasons. Thus refugees upon arriving in this country could be placed in internment camps similar to those used for the Japanese on the West Coast and released only after a satisfactory investigation. Furthermore, even if we took these refugees and treated them as prisoners of war it would be better than letting them die.

Representative [Samuel] Dickstein stated in the House [of Representatives] on December 15 [1943]:

If we consider the fact that the average admission would then be at the rate of less than 50,000 per year, it is clear that the organs of our Government have not done their duty. The existing quotas call for the admission of more than 150,000 every year, so that if the quotas themselves had been filled there would have been a total of one-half million and not 500,000 during the period mentioned.

But that is not the whole story. There was no effect of any kind made to save from death many of the refugees who could have been saved during the time that transportation lines were available and there was no obstacle to their admission to the United States. But the obstructive policy of our organs of Government, particularly the State Department, which saw fit to hedge itself about with rules and regulations, instead of lifting rules and regulations, brought about a condition so that not even the existing immigration quotas are filled. . . .

The US Government Has Received Knowledge of the Situation in Europe

State Department officials not only have failed to facilitate the obtaining of information concerning Hitler's plans to exterminate the Jews of Europe but in their official capacity have gone so far as to surreptitiously attempt to stop the obtaining of information concerning the murder of the Jewish population in Europe.

The evidence supporting this conclusion is so shocking and so tragic that it is difficult to believe.

The facts are as follows:

Sumner Welles as Acting Secretary of State requests confirmation of Hitler's plan to exterminate the Jews. Having already received various reports on the plight of the Jews, on October 5, 1942, Sumner Welles as Acting Secretary of State sent a cable for the personal attention of [US] Minister [Leland] Harrison in Bern stating that leaders of the Jewish Congress had received reports from their representatives in Geneva and London to the effect that many thousands of Jews in Eastern Europe were being slaughtered pursuant to a policy embarked upon by the German Government for the complete extermination of the Jews in Europe. Welles added that he was trying to obtain further information from the Vatican but that other than this he was unable to secure confirmation of these stories. He stated that [Zionist leader] Rabbi [Stephen Samuel] Wise believed that information was available to his representatives in Switzerland but that they were in all likelihood fearful of dispatching any such reports through open cables or mail. He then stated that [World Jewish Congress representative in Geneva, Gerhart M.] Riegner and [Zionist leader Richard] Lichtheim were being requested by Wise to call upon Minister Harrison; and Welles requested Minister Harrison to advise him by telegram of all the evidence and facts which he might secure as a result of conference with Riegner and Lichtheim.

State Department receives confirmation and shocking evidence that the extermination was being rapidly and effectively carried out. Pursuant to Welles' cable of October 5 Minister Harrison forwarded documents from Riegner confirming the fact of extermination of the Jews (in November 1942), and in a cable of January 21, 1942, relayed a message from Riegner and Lichtheim which Harrison stated was for the information of the Under Secretary of State (and was to be transmitted to Rabbi Stephen Wise if the Under Secretary should so determine). This message described a horrible situation concerning the plight of Jews in Europe. It reported mass executions of Jews in Poland; according to one source 6,000 Jews were being killed daily; the Jews were required before execution to strip themselves of all their clothing, which was then sent to Germany; the remaining Jews in Poland were confined to ghettos, etc.; in Germany deportations were continuing; many Jews were in hiding and there had been many cases of suicide; Jews were being deprived of rationed foodstuffs; no Jews would be left in Prague or Berlin by the end of March, etc.; and in Rumania 130,000 Jews were deported to Transnistria; about 60,000 had already died and the remaining 70,000 were starving; living conditions were indescribable; Jews were deprived of all their money, foodstuffs and possessions; they were housed in deserted cellars, and occasionally twenty to thirty people slept on the floor of one unheated room; disease was prevalent, particularly fever; urgent assistance was needed.

Sumner Welles furnishes this information to the Jewish organizations. Sumner Welles furnished the documents received in November to the Jewish organizations in the United States and authorized them to make the facts public. On February 9, 1943, Welles forwarded the horrible message contained in [the] cable of January 21 to Rabbi Stephen Wise. In his letter of February 9 Welles stated that he was pleased to be of assistance in this matter.

The Spreading of Information Was Discouraged

Immediately upon the receipt of this message, the Jewish organizations arranged for a public mass meeting in Madison Square Garden in a further effort to obtain effective action.

Certain State Department officials surreptitiously attempt to stop this Government from obtaining further information from the very source from which the above evidence was received. On February 10, the day after Welles forwarded the message contained in [the] cable of January 21 to Rabbi Wise, and in direct response to this cable, a most highly significant cable was dispatched. This cable, of February 10, read as follows: . . .

> In the future we would suggest that you do not accept reports submitted to you to be transmitted to private persons in the United States unless such action is advisable because of extraordinary circumstances. Such private messages circumvent neutral

I am forced to conclude it is nothing less than an attempted suppression of information requested by this Government concerning the murder of Jews by Hitler.

countries' censorship and it is felt that by sending them we risk the possibility that steps would necessarily be taken by the neutral countries to curtail or forbid our means of communication for confidential official matter. . . .

Although this cable on its face is most innocent and innocuous, when read together with the previous cables, I am forced to conclude it is nothing less than an attempted suppression of information requested by this Government concerning the murder of Jews by Hitler.

Average Americans Knew of but Ignored the Plight of Jews in Europe

Ron Hollander

Much debate exists regarding newspaper coverage of the Holocaust during World War II and the extent to which the American public was aware of the atrocities that were being committed in Europe. In the viewpoint that follows, Ron Hollander presents extensive evidence to support his argument that US newspapers—both local and national—published explicit details about the violence being enacted against Jews in Europe. However, Americans, while aware of the facts, refused to speak out and force the government to intervene. He concludes that the unprecedented nature of the Holocaust, coupled with anti-Semitic sentiments, restrained American reaction. Hollander is a professor of English at Montclair State University in New Jersey and teaches a class on the Holocaust using newspaper reports from the period.

SOURCE. Ron Hollander, "We Knew: America's Newspapers Report the Holocaust," *Why Didn't the Press Shout?: American & International Journalism During the Holocaust.* Edited by Robert Moses Shapiro, Yeshiva University Press, 2003, pp. 41–48. Reproduced by permission.

*W*e knew.

Despite self-protective myths to the contrary, the American newspaper reading public during the Second World War knew early and in excruciatingly explicit detail of the systematic extermination of the Jews of Europe [the "Final Solution"].

This paper, excerpted from a forthcoming book, *We Knew: America's Newspapers Report the Holocaust*, surveying mainstream newspapers from 1941 to 1945 for their reporting of the Final Solution, documents that although coverage was inconsistent, news of the mass destruction of the Jews came early, prominently and widely to America.

America Should Acknowledge that the Public Knew About the Holocaust

At a time when the United States Holocaust Memorial Museum in Washington [D.C.] continues to break its own attendance projections, and *Schindler's List* [a 1993 film about a German businessman who saved Jewish refugees] has played even in China, amid America's self-congratulatory rhetoric on its role in "liberating" the concentration camps, it is well also to remember that *we knew*.

Not just in 1945 when we stumbled unpreparedly upon Dachau and Buchenwald [camps] while chasing the retreating Germans. But for at least the last three years of the war, while 3.5 million Jews were being murdered, *we knew*.

And not merely that the Jews of Europe were having a rough time. Or that tens or even hundreds of thousands had been shot, along with many others, by the indiscriminately brutal German occupiers.

But from 1942 on, we knew that the Germans were systematically exterminating specifically the Jews using gas chambers and crematoria. Nor was it just President Franklin Roosevelt and State Department officials with access to secret cables who knew. The American public itself read in its morning and evening papers that the Jews were being wiped out.

Reports after Liberation Express Shock

The myth that we have nurtured in the intervening half-century—and that was fostered at the time—is that Americans, the ordinary man and woman on the street, first learned of the Final Solution in April and May 1945, when Fox-Movietone newsreels showed the walking skeletons and the bodies stacked like cordwood.

> The myth that we have nurtured . . . is that Americans, the ordinary man and woman on the street, first learned of the Final Solution in April and May 1945.

"Nazi Bestiality Revealed" and "Nazi Murder Mills" intoned the narrators who in fact were not even describing the extermination camps of Poland, but the "mere" concentration camps of Germany.

Broadcasting for CBS from Buchenwald on April 15, 1945, [American journalist] Edward R. Murrow spoke as if he were breaking the news for the first time. "I pray you to believe what I have said about Buchenwald," Murrow begged his presumably skeptical audience. "Murder had been done at Buchenwald."

Three days later *The New York Times* reported from the camp, "Not until today has the full import of the atrocities been completely felt." General Dwight D. Eisenhower was so shocked by what he found in what several inmates described as the best concentration camp in Germany that he cabled home for senators and representatives to come see what he had discovered.

On April 22, 1945, Representatives Gordon Canfield of New Jersey and Henry "Scoop" Jackson of Washington, among others, toured Buchenwald. Two days later, Kentucky Senator and future Vice-President

Alben Barkley arrived. From all came stunned expressions of "we had no idea." *The Philadelphia Inquirer* four days later summed up this inexplicable shock with its headline, "Nazi Horrors Too Awful For Belief."

What else could America claim but that it knew only belatedly of the gas chambers and crematoria? If we acknowledge—even 50 years later—that we did know all along, then how to explain our failure to do anything, to drop intentionally even one bomb on Auschwitz-Birkenau when we were repeatedly bombing factories, including Auschwitz-Buna, only three miles away?

American Newspapers' Early Reports on Jewish Troubles

The reality is that by October 1941—two months before Pearl Harbor—the story of the Germans' so-called "resettlement" of the Jews was sent by the Associated Press to papers around the country. *The New York Times* said it straight out: "NAZIS SEEK TO RID EUROPE OF ALL JEWS."

And as early as June 1942, the mainstream American press printed stories—not infrequently on page 1—documenting the assembly-line murder of the Jews. Thus, on June 1, a paper as local as *The Seattle Daily Times* ran a bold, capitalized headline across the very top of page 1, above the paper's name: "JEWS SLAIN TOTAL 200,000!" Under the subhead, "MILLIONS DRIVEN TO GHETTOES," the United Press wire service story said, "Adolf Hitler's agents, in the most terrible racial persecution in modern history, have killed at least 200,000 Jews in Russia, Poland and the Baltic States." The article went on to remind readers that [Nazi leader Adolf] Hitler had prophesied to the Reichstag [German parliament] on January 30, 1939, that another world war would result in destruction of the Jews, "and correspondents know that his agents have done everything possible to make the prophecy come true."

Photo on following page: Rabbi Stephen Wise's high-profile wartime press conferences about the Nazis' mass murder of Jews went unheeded by most Americans. (**Associated Press.**)

On June 26, 1942, the *Boston Daily Globe* ran a page 12 story under a three-column headline making clear that the deaths were not random but were the implementation of a specific policy. "A systematic campaign for the extermination of the Jews in Poland has resulted in the murder of more than 700,000 in the past year" read the Overseas News Agency story filed from London.

Four days later, on June 30, 1942, *The New York Times* upped the death total to 1 million. In a modest, one-column story on page 7, the *Times* reported, "The Germans have massacred more than 1,000,000 Jews since the war began in carrying out Adolf Hitler's proclaimed policy of exterminating the people." The United Press account said, ". . . the Nazis had established a vast slaughterhouse for Jews in Eastern Europe" and that about one-sixth of the pre-war Jewish population in Europe of 6–7 million "had been wiped out in less than three years."

The *San Francisco Chronicle*'s version of the story added, "The slaughter is part of the Nazis' policy that 'physical extermination of the Jew must from now on be the aim of Germany and her allies.'" *The Philadelphia Inquirer* put the figure at 1.1 million in its page 3 headline.

> "The news [of the Holocaust] was there, but not always prominently or consistently displayed."

Many Newspaper Accounts of the Holocaust Were Buried

Although the news was often displayed prominently in the papers, it was just as often buried. The discrepancy between the enormity of the news—more than 1 million slaughtered—and the "play" *The New York Times* gave its six-paragraph story on page 7 under a tiny, one-column headline, embodies in microcosm the American press's coverage of the Holocaust. The news was there, but not always prominently or consistently displayed.

The stories—while covered—often were downplayed for many reasons. The Final Solution was carried out in secret, deep in German-held Poland, far from the eyes of foreign correspondents. The press had to rely on sources it felt were less verifiable, such as the Polish underground or even escapees from the camps, who were often skeptically regarded as exaggerating their stories to make the Jewish plight seem worse.

There was no precedent for the intentional, continent-wide extermination of a people, and that made the news hard to swallow for editors and readers alike. (Informed by Polish courier Jan Karski in 1943 of the ongoing destruction of the Jews, Supreme Court Justice Felix Frankfurter, himself Jewish, told Karski it wasn't that he didn't believe him, but that he couldn't.)

The extermination seemed especially illogical and thus unbelievable since in wartime a nation needed all the labor it could get. Why would the Germans kill off good Jewish workers? And why would they expend so much men and matériel to do it while fighting a two-front war? (Survivors have told of freight trains of Jews chugging through on the main line while troop trains loaded with tanks and weapons waited on sidings.)

Also, atrocities against Jews was an old story by the time of the war. The papers had carried enough such stories through the Thirties. (At one point, *Time* magazine referred cynically to the latest "'atrocity' story of the week.")

Finally, the press was wary of being suckered during World War II by tales of German atrocities as it had been during the First World War. In that time of the birth of modern propaganda, the papers were full of stories of Germans raping Belgian nuns, chaining them to machine guns and bayoneting babies. Most of them proved false, and when the press started hearing even more bizarre reports from the shrouded Eastern front, it was wary.

American Holocaust Guilt and the Creation of Israel

It is often assumed that feelings of guilt drove the United States to support the creation of the state of Israel in 1948. This is an easy conclusion to make, considering that Israel became a state just three years after the war. During those three years, Americans had the opportunity to view first-hand the horror of stacked corpses and emaciated human beings left behind in extermination camps. If Americans did feel at all responsible for the Holocaust, what better way to atone for its guilt than to push for a Jewish state for the victims who managed to survive? This is essentially what [American journalist] Dan Raviv and [Israeli journalist] Yossi Melman argue in *Friends in Deed: Inside the U.S.-Israel Alliance*. According to Raviv and Melman, as a result of the Holocaust "a shamefaced, remorseful postwar West now supported the Jewish demand for an independent state in Palestine."

It is unclear whether or not guilt was behind U.S. policy to support the creation of Israel. According to [American historian] Peter Novick in *The Holocaust in American Life*, there is no evidence President Harry Truman or his advisors ever felt guilty during their push for a Jewish state. Although Truman did show genuine concern for the survivors, probably also high on his list was the effect his support of Israel might have on his chances for reelection in 1948. In the case of U.S. policy toward Holocaust victims in general, Novick notes that no evidence points to a sense of guilt as motivation. According to Novick, "sympathy" is probably a better word to explain how Americans felt about the plight of Holocaust victims after the war. In later years, the government expressed sympathy for victims of genocide, such as the Rwandan genocide of 1994, and for victims of natural disasters, such as the Armenian earthquake of 1988, and chose to assist them; this sympathy was also at the root of U.S. assistance for Holocaust victims.

SOURCE. *James C. Mott, "Holocaust Guilt," Americans at War. Ed. John P. Resch. Vol. 4: 1946–Present. Detroit: Macmillan Reference, 2005.*

The Compelling Detail of Holocaust Coverage

Yet the bottom line is that spotty and de-emphasized as coverage might have been on occasion, it was there in compelling detail. As early as June 26, 1942, the Chicago Daily News Foreign Service sent a story from London that its subscriber newspapers across the country carried. The story reported, "Polish sources insist the Nazis are using portable gas chambers . . . at the village of Chelmno, where Jews were crowded 90 at a time into the chamber." (Chelmno, 90 miles west of Warsaw, was the first death camp to start gassing on December 8, 1941, ultimately killing about 300,000 Jews.)

If there was little reason to doubt by mid-1942 that the Jews were being exterminated, there was even less excuse after November and December. For then the news of the Final Solution was not only carried throughout America but was confirmed by the State Department. And the Holocaust was condemned officially by the Allies in an unequivocally clear declaration reported on page 1 of *The New York Times.*

> All the press's previous qualifying of its news reports because the underground sources were unverifiable was removed with the official imprimatur of the Allies' declaration of December 17, 1942.

On November 24 and 25, 1942, Rabbi Stephen S. Wise, head of the World Jewish Congress, held successive press conferences in Washington [D.C.] and New York, confirming details of the exterminations that had been smuggled out of Germany and Poland. Combined with similar information released at the same time by the Polish government-in-exile in London, the news was carried nationwide. The *Washington Post* ran the Associated Press story on November 25 on page 6: "2 Million Jews Slain, Rabbi Wise Asserts."

The *Washington Post*'s story reported that "Wise . . . said that he had learned through sources confirmed by the State Department that approximately half the estimated four million Jews in Nazi-occupied Europe had been slain in an 'extermination campaign.'" An accompanying article described the Jews being jammed into freight cars: "The people are packed so tightly that those who die of suffocation remain in the crowd side by side with those still living," wrote the Associated Press. "Those surviving are sent to special camps at Treblinka, Belzec and Sobibor [where] they are mass-murdered."

The *New York Herald Tribune* ran the story on the front page with a two-column headline that read: "Wise Says Hitler Has Ordered 4,000,000 Jews slain in 1942." In Colorado, the *Denver Post* eschewed the numbers game and simply said, "DEATH FOR EVERY JEW IN EUROPE IS CALLED NAZI GOAL." The *St. Louis Post-Dispatch* put the story at the top of page 1B with the 4 million figure in the headline.

On the same day, *The New York Times*—besides carrying the Wise information—reported that "concrete buildings on the former Russian frontiers are used by the Germans as gas chambers in which thousands of Jews have been put to death." The story detailed "methods by which the Germans in Poland are carrying out the slaughter of Jews [with] trainloads of adults and children taken to great crematoriums at Oswiecim near Krakow." The village of Oswiecim, a half-hour drive from the venerable university city of Krakow, was known to the Germans as Auschwitz.

Press Coverage Drives the Allies to Limited Action

The pressure of these accumulating reports at last forced the Allies to do officially and publicly what they had resisted doing for months: Acknowledge flat out that they knew the Jews were being exterminated. All the press's previous qualifying of its news reports because the underground sources were unverifiable was removed with the official imprimatur of the Allies' declaration of December 17, 1942.

Issued by the United States, England and the Soviet Union and the governments-in-exile of eight occupied countries, the declaration confirmed unequivocally Germany's "intention to exterminate the Jewish people in Europe" and condemned "this bestial policy of cold-blooded extermination."

In lieu of concrete action, the declaration pledged feebly that those responsible would be punished at the war's end. As late as June, 1944, when Jewish groups pleaded for the bombing of Auschwitz-Birkenau or of the rail line to it, the Allied response—even knowing that 12,000 Hungarian Jews a day were being gassed—was that the best way to help the Jews was to win the war and that nothing could be diverted for such "side shows." In the single most disgraceful American document of the war, Assistant Secretary of War John J. McCloy on August 14, 1944, rejected an appeal from the World Jewish Congress to bomb Auschwitz. McCloy's three-paragraph letter said that "such an effort . . . might provoke even more vindictive action by the Germans." Eleven days later McCloy had U.S. Army aerial photographs showing Jews actually lined up for the gas chambers, but he never relented.

The Allied declaration was carded widely. It was front-page news in *The New York Times*. It was on page 3 in the *San Francisco Examiner*, page 4 in the *Los Angeles Times*, page 2 in the *Atlanta Constitution* and page 10 in the *Washington Post*. Other major papers carrying the declaration—though farther back—included the *St. Louis Post-Dispatch*, the *Los Angeles Examiner* and the *New York World Telegram*.

Americans Admit that They Knew About the Holocaust

More stories followed, and in January 1943, a Gallup poll asked whether it was true that 2 million Jews had already been murdered. With two years' worth of news reports still to come, almost half of those polled said it was true. The others said they didn't know or that the report was just a rumor.

A year later, in December 1944, the *Washington Post* carried the results of another Gallup poll that showed that 76 percent of those questioned believed that "many people" had been murdered in German concentration camps.

Newspaper readers of the time recall the clarity of the reports even today. "The news was there for all to see," said camp "liberator" Vito Farese, 67, of Short Hills, New Jersey, interviewed by the author in April, 1993. A GI [soldier] drafted in late 1943, he eventually reached Mauthausen and Flossenburg concentration camps. "There's no question in my mind," he said. "You would have to have been pretty oblivious not to know that extermination was being committed. People just turned their backs."

A Reason Why Americans Turned Their Heads

Many reasons account for that. The Holocaust was without precedent. The numbers were staggering. Who could believe that the nation of [writers Friedrich] Schiller and [Johan Wolfgang von] Goethe was gassing even 2 million Jews? Strictly military news took precedence. Editors and readers followed correspondents' eye-witness accounts of the progress of armies and the outcomes of battles, not murky reports of civilian deaths in bizarre circumstances.

Anti-Semitism, too, played a role. In June 1944, a poll asked which groups constituted the greatest "threat" to America. With the war in the Pacific having more than a bloody year still to run, with Ameri-

> Journalists no less than ordinary citizens suffered temporary amnesia when it came to the Holocaust.

cans fighting the Germans in Normandy, and with more than 4.5 million Jews already dead, 6 percent of those polled said the Germans posed the greatest threat to America. Nine percent said it was the Japanese. And 24 percent of those queried said that the greatest threat to America was posed by the Jews!

An Indictment of the American Moral Will to Act

That the extermination of the Jews was reported in detail long before 1945 is incontrovertible. That many learned the news and consciously or not chose to reject it is also true. Journalists no less than ordinary citizens suffered temporary amnesia when it came to the Holocaust. Perhaps the moral consequences of having known and of having done nothing were too great to integrate into the American self-image.

Yet that is the irrefutable, disquieting legacy bequeathed us by America's yellowing newspapers from more than 50 years ago. They constitute an indictment not merely of official American foreign policy, but of mass American moral will to speak up and to act. The more the horrors were revealed, the more firmly did we say, "We didn't know; our hands are clean." Unfortunately, it is not so simple to rewrite history, especially not when the newspapers are there to rebuke us. This is the unwanted bequest to us of the past. We would do well to be guided by it as we survey the world in the present.

Many Germans Had No Choice but to Participate in Nazi Schemes

Max von Laue

Max von Laue, a Nobel Prize-winning German scientist, was known throughout the Nazi Party's reign to be openly opposed to the politics and actions of the National Socialists. In addition, he aided many Jewish German scientists to emigrate from the country so they could be safe from Nazi policies. In the following article, von Laue responds to an American who criticizes German scientists as a group for conducting scientific studies on behalf of the Nazis during the Holocaust. The American, however, lauds von Laue for remaining "aloof from the German war efforts." Von Laue retorts that many scientists were forced to work for the war effort against their will and that these scientists were often able to aid others who would otherwise have been killed by giving them jobs conducting research. Von Laue concludes stating that pointing fingers at Germans and others

SOURCE. Max von Laue, "The Wartime Activities of German Scientists," *Bulletin of the Atomic Scientists*, April 1948, pp. 103. Reproduced by permission.

who were coerced into certain actions during the war does little to ease the transition into peacetime relations between the individuals and countries formerly on opposite sides during the conflict.

In the *Bulletin of the Atomic Scientists* for December 1947, Philip Morrison, in a review of [Samuel Abraham] Goudsmit's book *Alsos*, writes as follows:

> The documents cited in *Alsos* prove amply, that no different from their Allied counterparts, the German scientists worked for the military as best their circumstances allowed. But the difference, which it will be never possible to forgive, is that they worked for the cause of [Nazi military commander Heinrich] Himmler and Auschwitz [a concentration camp] for the burners of books and the takers of hostages. The community of science will be long delayed in welcoming the armorers of the Nazis, even if their work was not successful. Men were able to remain aloof from the German war efforts, and brave and good men like [Max von] Laue and [nuclear physicist Wolfgang] Gentner could resist the Nazis even in the sphere of science. That is a story *Alsos* does not fully tell.

At the time of writing we have not yet seen the book itself. One concludes however from the above quotation that it is the reviewer who explicitly puts forward the monstrous suggestion that German scientists as a body worked for Himmler and Auschwitz. How far Morrison has suffered personally through both or either is unknown to us. We do know that Goudsmit lost not only father and mother, but many near relatives as well, in Auschwitz and other concentration camps. We realize fully what unutterable pain the mere word Auschwitz must always evoke in him. But for that very reason we can recognize neither him, nor his reviewer Morrison,

German physicist Max von Laue, who saved Jewish scientists' lives, writes that many of his colleagues worked under Nazi duress. (**Hulton Archive/ Getty Images.**)

as capable of an unbiased judgment of the particular circumstances of the present case. Accordingly a few words in protest may be allowed us here.

Scientific Cooperation Saved Lives

Ever since war between civilized states relapsed once more into the old barbaric "total" war between peoples, it has been no easy matter for an isolated citizen of a warring nation to withdraw himself altogether from war service; indeed, it is relatively unimportant whether he puts his heart into such war service, or whether he is opposed to the methods of his government, or even whether he would depose it. If one or other among the German scientists found it possible during the war to avoid being drawn with his work into the maelstrom, it is not allowable to conclude that it was so for all.

> If one or other among the German scientists found it possible during the war to avoid being drawn with his work into the maelstrom, it is not allowable to conclude that it was so for all.

The directors of the larger research institutes in particular were under the absolute necessity of putting the facilities of their institutes at least partially and formally at the service of the war effort. Open refusal on their part, immediately classable as "sabotage", would have led inexorably to catastrophic consequences to themselves. On the other hand, an (often fictitious) compliance with the demands of the armed forces had advantages which our opponents should recognize as legitimate. In particular one could in this way shield a quite considerable number of the younger specialists from a much more direct mobilization for war; and by this and several other means preserve throughout the war years the foundation on which now, *after* the war, we seek to build afresh.

Sometimes too the possibility arose of protecting political suspects from concentration camps or worse, by assigning them research work of more or less "military importance". Our severer critics might perhaps inquire about such cases among non-Aryan Germans (there were a few such in Germany even during the war). Or do they wish to declaim even in these cases about "armorers of Himmler and Auschwitz"?

Nevertheless: whosoever put his institute in this fashion at the disposal of the military authorities, put himself in an ambiguous position. That is the particular curse of such a time: and it visited not Germans only. Thus a foreign colleague, who during the occupation of his fatherland by [Nazi leader Adolf] Hitler's troops had been particularly active in the underground movement, told me recently that the double dealing to which he was forced thereby lays him open even yet among many of his compatriots to the suspicion of collaboration. This example illustrates how careful one must be in passing judgment on events which took place under a tyranny.

German Scientists Return to Peacetime Research

Part of the answer to the question which asks what German scientists were actually about during the war is given in the 50-odd volumes of the *Fiat* Reviews of German Science 1939–46, now in course of publication. There one may find, not perhaps world shaking results, but honest, solid scientific investigation, following steadily in the steps of the preceding peacetime research, now once more resumed. Admittedly, the scientific journals lapsed, one after another, towards the end of the war; but not for lack of work submitted for publication, but because of paper shortages, bomb damage to printing houses, and other economic strictures. In the case of the [German physics journal] *Zeitschrift für Physik*, for instance, where I know the circumstances at first hand, there were 60 manuscripts awaiting publication at the end of the war; since when the editors could have accepted 86 more, which still deal, to a considerable extent, with work carried out during the war years. But nothing in their contents points to that fact; and they have verily nothing whatsoever to do with Himmler and Auschwitz.

What do the "Atomic Scientists" aim at in their Bulletin? So far as I understand it, the attainment of a durable peace. But that high aim is ill served by articles such as the review from which we have quoted; they keep alive hate, on the elimination of which *everything* hinges. We recommend as the foundation of every utterance of peace politics, in great and small things alike, the words which [ancient Greek playwright] Sophocles puts in the mouth of [tragic character] Antigone, citizeness of a victorious state: "To league with love not hatred was I born".

German Perpetrators of the Holocaust Participated Willingly in the Torture and Murder of Jews

Daniel Jonah Goldhagen

Much of the controversy surrounding the Holocaust has revolved around the issue of why "ordinary" Germans participated in or silently ignored the mass slaughter of Jewish people throughout Europe. In the viewpoint that follows, an American author and former professor of government and social studies, Daniel Jonah Goldhagen, argues that the German people who committed atrocities against Jews during the Holocaust did so as a result of a fervent hatred and a desire to inflict pain and suffering on them. Goldhagen contends that contrary to many critics' views, these Germans were fully aware of their actions,

SOURCE. Daniel Jonah Goldhagen, "Motives, Causes, and Alibis," *New Republic* 215 (26), December 23, 1996, pp. 37–45. Reproduced by permission.

passed on chances to refrain from the brutality, and possessed many of the same characteristics as other perpetrators of genocide. Goldhagen is well-known for his book *Hitler's Willing Executioners*, a treatise on his belief in the guilt of average Germans.

At the end of March [1996], my book *Hitler's Willing Executioners: Ordinary Germans and the Holocaust* was published, with several unexpected results. I did not anticipate that a scholarly book would become a best-seller not only in the United States but also in Germany and a half dozen other countries, or that it would produce so much discussion here and abroad. I expected that the book would receive criticism, since it argues that central aspects of our understanding of the Holocaust need to be revised, but I was taken by surprise by the vitriolic and sometimes wild nature of some of the critics' writings.

Ordinary Germans Believed Jews Should Be Killed

The book shows that the German perpetrators were ordinary Germans coming from all social backgrounds who formed a representative sample of adult Germans in their age groups; that not a small number of Germans, but a bare minimum of 100,000 Germans and probably many more, were perpetrators; and that these ordinary Germans were, by and large, willing, even eager executioners of the Jewish people, including Jewish children. It also shows that the eliminationist anti-Semitism that moved these ordinary Germans was extremely widespread in German society during and even before the Nazi period. The basic eliminationist anti-Semitic model held that Jews were different from Germans; that these putative differences resided in their biology, conceptualized as race, and were therefore immutable; that the Jews were evil and powerful, had done great harm to Germany and would continue to do so. The conclusion drawn by Germans who shared this view was that Jews and Jewish power had to be eliminated somehow if Germany was to be secure and to prosper. The German perpetrators of the Holocaust were motivated to kill Jews principally by their belief that the extermination was necessary and just.

That is the core argument of my book, an argument that is grounded in extensive research on the perpetrators, particularly their own testimonies as given to the authorities of the Federal Republic during postwar legal investigations and trials. It is the perpetrators themselves who tell us of their voluntarism in the slaughter, of their routine brutalities against helpless Jewish victims, of their degrading and mocking of the Jews. It is they who tell us of their boasting, their celebrations, their memorializations of their deeds, including not the least of which are the many photographs which they took, passed around, put in their albums and sent home to loved ones. This record of the perpetrators' own words and photographic images forms the empirical basis of my book and its conclusions. . . .

Restoring the Notion of Individual Responsibility

Thousands of books, monographs and articles have been written on Nazism and the Holocaust. Yet the questions of why many tens of thousands of ordinary Germans from all walks of life, Nazis and non-Nazis alike, killed, tortured and degraded Jews with zeal and energy, and why only a minuscule number availed themselves of the opportunities to withdraw from the unimaginably gruesome killing, have scarcely been broached by historians. Most would agree that these are questions of great importance, that no explanation of the Holocaust can be called adequate if it does not contain satisfying answers to them. . . .

Photo on following page: Grisly "souvenirs," like this shrunken human head created by Nazis from a victim's remains, were introduced at the Nuremberg tribunals as evidence of German hatred for Jews. (Associated Press.)

My book goes against the grain of many (though not all) [of] the critics' outlooks and of the existing literature on the Holocaust. It shifts the focus of the investigation away from impersonal institutions and abstract structures (which is where it has overwhelmingly been located) directly onto the actors—onto the human beings who committed the crimes and onto the populace from which these people came. And this forces people to come to grips with the most central and troubling questions of the Holocaust.

> My analysis is predicated upon the recognition that each individual made choices about how to treat Jews. It therefore restores the notion of individual responsibility.

I acknowledge the humanity of the actors in a specific manner that others do not. My book eschews the ahistorical, universal explanations of social psychology—such as the notions that people obey all authority, or that they will do anything under peer pressure—that are often invoked, against so much evidence, when accounting for the perpetrators' actions. Instead, I recognize that the perpetrators were not automatons or puppets but individuals who had beliefs and values about the wisdom of the regime's policies which informed the choices that these individuals, alone and together, made. My analysis is predicated upon the recognition that each individual made choices about how to treat Jews. It therefore restores the notion of individual responsibility.

My book also takes seriously the real historical context in which the German perpetrators developed their beliefs and values about the world, beliefs and values that were critical for their understanding of what was right and necessary in the treatment of Jews. For these reasons, it is imperative to learn as much as possible about the German perpetrators' views of their victims and about the choices that they made, as well as about the views of Jews that were generally present in their society. This leads to two sets of questions central to the understanding of the Holocaust. The first set of questions is about the perpetrators: What did they believe about Jews? Did they look upon them as a dangerous, evil enemy or as innocent human beings who were being treated unjustly? Did they believe that their treatment of the Jews was right and necessary? And, if so, why? The second set of questions is about Germans during the Nazi period: How many were anti-Semites? What was the character of their anti-Semitism? What did they think of the anti-Jewish measures of the 1930s? What did they know about and think of the extermination of Jews? . . .

The Extreme Brutality of the Holocaust

The purpose of the central investigation of my book is to uncover and explain the perpetrators' pattern of actions, which includes the pattern of their choices. This enterprise, which is informed by the methodology of the social sciences, should be recognized as the primary explanatory task when studying the perpetrators. I have been able to adopt this approach because, against the existing accounts of the perpetrators, I accept the premise upon which it depends, namely the recognition that individuals are responsible agents who make choices. . . .

For it is not just the killing that needs to be explained, but also something which others have not recognized: the virtually limitless cruelty that the perpetrators inflicted upon their victims and that was a constituent feature of the Holocaust, as central to it as the killing itself. As the testimonies of survivors show, and as the killers with their testimonies themselves confirm, the perpetrators brutalized Jews in the extreme. This brutality had no utilitarian purpose. It was—and this needs to be emphasized again and again—nearly ubiquitous, inflicted by the overwhelming majority of Germans who had direct and extensive contact with Jews. To beat and to degrade

Sempo Sugihara: Japanese Holocaust Rescuer

Sempo Sugihara was the Japanese consul at Kovno (present-day Kaunas, in Lithuania). When the city fell to German expansion and was made part of Poland, Sugihara became aware of the Jewish plight in the summer of 1940. For humanitarian reasons, Sugihara issued Japanese transit visas to Jewish refugees without checking the validity of their supporting documents. The holders of such visas could travel to Japan through the Soviet Union if they were able to pay the fare in U.S. dollars for the trip across Siberia. When the Japanese foreign ministry learned about Sugihara's aid to Jews, they ordered him to stop, but Sugihara continued to issue visas. He worked non-stop for twelve consecutive days, enlisting the help of Jewish refugees, and he was still issuing visas while boarding his train for Berlin, on August 31. Sugihara estimated that he had distributed 3,500 transit visas.

In Tokyo, Sugihara was fired. He had a hard time finding work, and was forced to move from one job to another. Only in 1985, old and bedridden, when Sugihara was officially designated by Yad Vashem as a "Righteous Among the Nations," did the Japanese press give extensive coverage to his selfless wartime aid to Jews.

SOURCE. *Nechama Tec, "Rescuers, Holocaust,"* Encyclopedia of Genocide and Crimes Against Humanity. *Ed. Dinah L. Shelton. Vol. 2. Detroit: Macmillan Reference, 2005.*

Jews was, among their German keepers, normative. As the head woman guard of one death march at the very end of the war testified, even though the guards had received direct orders not to kill and torture the emaciated, sick and dying Jewish women, all of the German women guards "carried rods and all of them beat the [Jewish] girls."

Why were the Jews not put to death in the same manner in which common criminals are executed? Why did ordinary Germans not act as modern hangmen do, who administer death in a prescribed quasi-clinical manner, swiftly, without torment and with minimum pain—in the manner in which the ordinary Germans who killed the mentally ill and others in the so-called Euthanasia program sometimes made efforts to kill? The ordinary German perpetrators of the Holocaust, by contrast, routinely sought to inflict maximum pain on Jews. This, and much other evidence from the Nazi period, and from other historical instances of mass killing, shows that such cruelty is not integral to the task of killing, but that the frequency, the character and the intensity of perpetrators' cruelty vary greatly with the perpetrators' conception of the victims. Even if Germans had not killed millions of Jews, the amount of sustained, inventive, wanton, voluntary cruelty and degradation that they inflicted upon the Jews would be seen as one of the great crimes in history and would in itself demand an explanation. Yet no historian has thought it necessary to put this phenomenon at the center of study.

> Even if Germans had not killed millions of Jews, the amount of sustained, inventive, wanton, voluntary cruelty and degradation that they inflicted upon the Jews would be seen as one of the great crimes in history.

My emphasis on the perpetrators' cruelty is fundamental in three respects. It shows that any explanation of the perpetration of the Holocaust that leaves out this constituent feature is fundamentally inadequate. In the

> By the time Hitler came to power, the model of Jews that was the basis of his anti-Semitism was shared by the vast majority of Germans.

language of social science, it shifts the dependent variable, namely, the kinds of actions and outcomes that must be explained. And it drives the central task of the book, namely to explain the actions of the perpetrators. My assertion about the centrality of the perpetrators' cruelty is essential both for assessing the character and conclusions of my study and for how we conceive of the Holocaust. . . .

Germans Shared Anti-Semitic Sentiments

Turning now to my account of anti-Semitism: I argue that an eliminationist form of anti-Semitism became extremely widespread in Germany already in the nineteenth century. By the time [Nazi leader Adolf] Hitler came to power, the model of Jews that was the basis of his anti-Semitism was shared by the vast majority of Germans. That is why Hitler succeeded with frightening ease in accomplishing the task that he had proclaimed in one of his earliest speeches (August 13, 1920) of converting Germans' hitherto inactive anti-Semitic sentiments into a genocidal impetus. Hitler declared that the "broad masses" of Germans possess an "instinctive" anti-Semitism. His task consisted in "waking, whipping up, and inflaming the instinctive [anti-Semitism] in our Volk" until "it decides to join the movement which is ready to draw from it the [necessary] consequence" and that consequence, he intimated elsewhere in the speech, ought to be the death penalty for that "parasitical people."

My conclusions about German anti-Semitism follow from my conceptualization of the nature of anti-Semitism, which the critics do not bother to mention, namely that a culturally shared model of Jews held them to be unalterably different from Germans and dangerous, and that, therefore, they had to be eliminated somehow if Germany were to be secure and prosper. Whatever the differences that existed in the pernicious qualities that different Germans (including Austrians) attributed to Jews in their accounts of the putative Jewish danger, it is this model that is crucial for understanding the readiness of Germans to support and take part in the eliminationist measures of the 1930s and 1940s. . . .

All Genocide Perpetrators Have Common Motivation

I maintain that the perpetrators who, uncoerced, chose to mock, degrade, torture and kill other people, and to celebrate and memorialize their deeds, did so because they hated their victims, held them to be guilty and believed that they were right to treat them in these ways. The position of all those who say that I am wrong is that people who acted in these ways did so even though they did not hate their victims, even though they held them to be innocent, and even though they did not believe that they were right to do so. In the face of the perpetrators' volunteering, their acts of torture, their zeal and energy in killing Jews, their celebrations of the deaths, and their testimony to all of this, what do phrases like "peer pressure" have to do with the reality of the Holocaust? What does it have to do with the reality of the ordinary Germans in Police Battalion 309 wantonly rounding up and then burning to death hundreds of defenseless Jews in the great synagogue of Bialystok? In a remark uncharacteristic for the alleged reluctant killer who had never been "brutalized" because this was his first contact with the fantasized enemy, one of the genocidal killers exulted: "Let it burn, it's a nice little fire [schones Feuerlein], it's great fun." How does "peer pressure," in the sense of reluctantly carrying out a task that one condemns because one supposedly does not want to let down one's buddies, get translated into the reality of the virtually boundless, unnecessary, collective suffering of the Jews at the hands of the ordinary German perpetrators who, as one survivor puts it, "always came to us with whips and dogs"?

The oddness of the critics' view of the perpetrators is set in sharp relief when seen from another perspective. When people think about any other mass slaughter or genocide, in Rwanda, in the former Yugoslavia, in Turkey, in Cambodia, people naturally assume that the killers believed that what they were doing was right. Indeed, in these and other instances of large-scale mass slaughter, as in the Soviet Union or the massacre of the Indonesian Communist Party, it is recognized that the two necessary genocidal conditions that I mentioned earlier—a perpetrator group that hates the victim group and a political leadership bent upon mass killing—have been present. The only perpetrators of genocide or mass slaughter about whom people routinely assert the opposite, namely that they did not believe that they were right to kill, are the German perpetrators of the Holocaust.

> The victims remember the perpetrators bristling with hatred of Jews and killing them with joy.

This odd situation cries out for an explanation, which might be demanded of all who propagate it. I am saying that, in this sense, the German perpetrators were like the perpetrators of other mass slaughters. It is the denial of this—against so much evidence—that is curious, that should be controversial. . . .

Cohesion Between Survivor and Perpetrator Testimony

The reception of my argument among survivors of the Holocaust is also worth noting. Many have affirmed to me that the ordinary Germans with whom they came into contact were, with some exceptions, not mere obeyers of orders or coldly uninvolved executioners, as so many historians have argued. The victims remember the perpetrators bristling with hatred of Jews and killing them with joy. This is a common theme of the vast body of books, memoirs and testimonies of the survivors.

Indeed, one of the serious omissions of much of the historiography of the perpetration of the Holocaust (but not, obviously, of the historiography that focuses on the plight of the Jews) is its failure to draw on the accounts and the testimonies of the victims. Slaves and victims of violence and repression are indispensable witnesses. They can tell us whether their victimizers acted with gusto or reluctantly, with relish or with restraint, whether they abused their victims verbally or performed their tasks with detached taciturnity. No historian would dare write of the conduct of American slave masters without drawing on the available accounts of slaves. Yet many historians of the perpetrators of the Holocaust and of Nazism rarely, if ever, listen to the voices of Jews recounting the manner of their treatment at the hands of the ordinary German practitioners of the Holocaust. . . . As my book reveals, the respective accounts of the survivors and of the perpetrators regarding the willingness, the zeal and the cruelty of the perpetrators actually often reinforce one another.

Ordinary Germans' Participation in the Holocaust Is a Product of Human Nature

Christopher R. Browning

Many explanations of the Holocaust treat Germany following World War I as a unique society fraught with predispositions and special circumstances that facilitated the growth and spread of the National Socialist Party and the Nazis' murderous policies toward Jews. In the following viewpoint, however, Christopher R. Browning refutes this notion and argues that there is something innate in all humans that would allow them to become perpetrators of genocide. Browning maintains that human nature itself is the essential ingredient that, when combined with the existing conditions in Germany, caused Germans to participate in atrocities against their fellow Jewish citizens. He contends that all humans are subject to complying with orders given by those they see as legitimate authority. So, when Germans were told

SOURCE. Christopher R. Browning, "Human Nature, Culture, and the Holocaust," *Chronicle of Higher Education*, October 18, 1996, pp. A72. Reproduced by permission of the author.

to perpetrate crimes against the Jewish community, they did so as a result of this urge to comply not out of a hatred that they uniquely felt for Jewish people. Browning is an American historian and author of the book *Ordinary Men: Reserve Police Battalion 101 and the Final Solution in Poland*.

In the summer of 1946—scarcely 15 months after his liberation from the Buchenwald concentration camp—an 18-year-old Jewish survivor named Abe Kimmelman spoke for several hours into the primitive tape recorder of an American psychologist studying trauma. Mr. Kimmelman's transcribed remarks subsequently filled 128 double-spaced typed pages. He continually addressed the question that never ceased to haunt him during the Holocaust: "What really is a human being?"

Historians Focus on Germany

In his own way, Mr. Kimmelman was posing the crucial question: How could human beings have perpetrated the Holocaust? By and large, historians have sought to answer that question by looking at German institutions and culture, anti-Semitism, and the traumatic effect of World War I on Germany. But they have shied away from addressing questions about human nature, which would require them to adopt an interdisciplinary approach.

For example, [American author and professor] Daniel Jonah Goldhagen's recent [1996] controversial book, *Hitler's Willing Executioners: Ordinary Germans and the Holocaust*, sought to explain the behavior of perpetrators of the Holocaust as the product of a particular German culture. Because all German society saw the world through the cognitive lens of "eliminationist" anti-Semitism, he claimed, virtually all Germans were "of one mind" with [Nazi leader Adolf] Hitler about the Jews and "wanted to be genocidal executioners."

Such an approach emphasizes both uniformity among Germans and a sharp difference between Germans and other people. Indeed, Dr. Goldhagen advised scholars to approach the Germans as if they were as alien to us as the Aztecs [an ancient Mexican civilization], who believed that human sacrifice was necessary to cause the sun to rise.

Imagining Holocaust Perpetrators as Human Beings

Abe Kimmelman took a different approach. He focused not on the particularities of German culture, but on universal characteristics of human nature. He didn't just talk about the Germans, for the perpetrators whom he encountered were of several nationalities, including Poles and Ukrainians. Mr. Kimmelman also was haunted by the behavior of the Jewish police in his Silesian hometown of Dabrowa Gornicza [a city in the historical region of Silesia, located primarily in Poland] and of several of the Jewish *kapos* (privileged prisoners used to control other prisoners) in the Silesian labor camp of Markstadt.

> Instead of treating the perpetrators of the Holocaust as utterly alien and different, [one survivor] assumed that they were human beings like himself, and he dared to imagine what he would have done in their place.

Mr. Kimmelman knew perfectly well that the whole diabolical system of the Holocaust traced back to "the policy of the Germans." But assigning historical responsibility didn't preclude understanding the frailty of human nature. Instead of treating the perpetrators of the Holocaust as utterly alien and different, Mr. Kimmelman assumed that they were human beings like himself, and he dared to imagine what he would have done in their place: "Today one can say if one does not want to be truthful, 'Yes, I definitely would have refused. I would never have taken such a dirty job.' But one can never be sure. . . . Because a human being is only a human being." In their capacity to do "horrible things," Mr. Kimmelman concluded, "all people are alike. There are only a few heroes."

The Conditions of the Nazis' Popularity

I am much more comfortable with Mr. Kimmelman's approach than one that sees the Germans as utterly different from other people. I believe that pre-war Germany was an integral part of European civilization. I also believe that it was the deep social, political, and ideological divisions splitting German society that made democracy unworkable and paved the way for the National Socialist [Nazi] minority to come to power.

In the last free election of the period, in November 1932, the Nazis received 33 percent of the vote, while the Communists and Socialists—bitter enemies of each other as well as of the Nazis—together got 37 percent. The Nazi regime gained broad popular support and legitimacy only after coming to power. As the historian William Sheridan Allen concluded in his classic case study, *The Nazi Seizure of Power: The Experience of a Single German Town, 1922–1945*, even in a highly Nazified town like Northeim, most people "were drawn to anti-Semitism because they were drawn to Nazism, not the other way around."

What allowed the Nazis to mobilize and harness the rest of society to the mass murder of European Jewry? Here I think that we historians need to turn to the insights of social psychology—the study of psychological reactions to social situations. Like Abe Kimmelman, we must ask, What really is a human being? We must give up the comforting and distanc-

> Individuals comply with the policies and orders of people whom they perceive as legitimate authorities in diverse ways.

ing notion that the perpetrators of the Holocaust were fundamentally a different kind of people because they were products of a radically different culture.

The Power of Legitimate Authority

One insightful example of the social-psychological approach is *Crimes of Obedience: Toward a Social Psychology of Authority and Responsibility*, by the psychologist Herbert C. Kelman and the sociologist V. Lee Hamilton. It is a study of "sanctioned massacre" that focused on the Mylai Massacre of 1968 [in which a US Army unit killed hundreds of South Vietnamese civilians], but it also shed considerable light on a key issue relevant to the study of perpetrators of the Holocaust—the relationship between legitimate authority, individual belief, and murderous behavior.

In these authors' view, legitimate authority may reside at three levels: in the political system of the nation state in general (government), in the individuals making policy and issuing orders (the commanders), and in the specific policies and orders themselves. Both situation and culture shape perceptions of, and responses to, legitimate authority.

For example, in military-type units in wartime, the authoritative weight of the state and commander is at its maximum, and the capacity of individuals to question or challenge the legitimacy of particular policies and orders is at a minimum. And prior hostility toward a target group helps dehumanize victims, enhancing a person's readiness to perpetrate massacres sanctioned by authority.

According to the authors, individuals comply with the policies and orders of people whom they perceive as legitimate authorities in diverse ways. One is nominal compliance—people conform in public but would not do so if no one were observing them. (In the context of perpetrators of the Holocaust, this would include people

Photo on following page: Jewish women in Linz, Austria, are exhibited in public, during Kristallnacht. Some argue that scapegoating and worse acts under Nazi rule are more common than many people want to believe. **(Getty Images.)**

134

who obeyed orders to kill, but stopped when not being supervised.)

A second way in which people comply with orders is by identifying with the model behavior expected of a particular position, such as soldier, policeman, or guard. Such behavior is accepted as binding both in public and in private, regardless of personal feelings. (This would include people who accepted the fact that in their roles as policemen and soldiers, they had to be "tough" enough to carry out executions when ordered, and did so dutifully, even when unhappy about it.)

In a third form of compliance, people internalize and come to share the values of the state or commander who is issuing orders. (The killers believed the victims should die and thus killed with conviction and zeal.)

All of these forms of compliance are "willing" in the sense that they are in response to the perceived legitimacy—rather than the coercive power—of authority.

The Evidence of the Power of Legitimate Authority

In my research into the postwar testimony of members of one German killing unit, Reserve Police Battalion 101, I found all three types of compliance. Looking at the same testimony, Dr. Goldhagen saw only one response—shared values and killing out of conviction—because he dismissed as mendacious any testimony that suggested that people had acted for other motives. In effect, his methodology guaranteed confirmation of his hypothesis that German killers acted only out of anti-Semitic beliefs, because it rejected virtually all evidence to the contrary.

Certainly there is no lack of evidence about Holocaust perpetrators whose beliefs and actions—hatred and murder of Jews—were congruent; but the hatred may not always have caused the murder.

As the psychologist James E. Waller pointed out in an article in the Spring 1996 issue of the journal *Holo-*

caust and Genocide Studies, behavior may shape belief just as belief may shape behavior. For example, people who started out responding to legitimate authority with an attitude of nominal compliance could well become true believers in what they were doing, through the natural desire to reduce the discrepancy between internal feelings and external acts. In short, once under way, a mass-murder program can gain momentum as perpetrators become true believers in what they are ordered to do.

> Any attempt to understand perpetrators of the Holocaust . . . requires an investigation of human nature.

In my own research, I found men in the police battalion who were transformed into enthusiastic killers as they participated in the Holocaust. Indeed, if even some Jewish policemen and *kapos* internalized attitudes consistent with behavior induced by extreme duress, as survivors such as Abe Kimmelman observed they did, how much more frequently must this have been the case for the German perpetrators?

Connecting Human Nature with the Holocaust Is Necessary

If history is made by human beings, and if human behavior is in turn shaped by differing cultures and histories—as well as by common instincts and propensities—both the questions posed by Kimmelman about human nature and those by Dr. Goldhagen about German culture are legitimate and necessary. But positing that the Germans were so fundamentally different from other Europeans that they shared a single, aberrant outlook and a uniform response to authority is not plausible.

Any attempt to understand perpetrators of the Holocaust—not just Germans, but all those recruited into its machinery of destruction—requires an investigation of human nature. We will add little to our ability to understand either the Holocaust or the events of killing and genocide reported on the front pages of our daily newspapers if we ignore that task.

Holocaust Revisionism Denies the Real Pain and Suffering Experienced by Millions

Barry Bennett

In the following viewpoint, Barry Bennett is appalled that postwar generations in the United States seem to know little about the Holocaust. He remarks that the vast ignorance of this terrible tragedy unfortunately allows revisionist rhetoric to compete with historical fact. Bennett claims that Holocaust deniers have their views aired in the press and on the Internet, ensuring that their prejudice enters reasoned debate and making it appear as legitimate as the overwhelming evidence that bears out the reality of the Nazi's Final Solution. Bennett maintains that the only way to rebut the claims of Holocaust deniers is to continue to teach the truth so that the horrors will not fade from the world's collective memory. Bennett is an attorney and an instructor at the University of Portland in Oregon.

SOURCE. Barry Bennett, "The Holocaust: Denial and Memory," *Humanist*, May-June 1997, pp. 6–8. Reproduced by permission of the author.

*T*hey caught Eichmann."

My mother flew into the kitchen, hissing an epithet through tight lips—a mixed curse and hosanna that reverberated against the knotty pine walls. I was sitting at the kitchen table with our neighbor and my mother's best friend Audrey, who gasped in response. The Israeli government had just announced that twelve days earlier it had captured Adolf Eichmann, overseer of the Final Solution, who had been hiding in Argentina since the end of World War II. It was May 23, 1960. I was seven years old.

These three words were my introduction to the Holocaust, [Nazi leader] Adolf Hitler's almost successful plan to murder all the Jews in Europe. Although I did not understand them, their combined vitriol and triumph have seared my memory like a brand. My mother died in 1973, before the onslaught of Holocaust revisionism, which denies the existence of the death camps and attributes the memory of the Holocaust to yet another Jewish conspiracy. Although she never heard the revisionist claims, I do not have to wonder what her reaction would have been.

> In a 1993 Roper poll, one-third of adults agreed it was possible that the Holocaust never happened.

Ignorance of the Holocaust

I don't remember our visits to the Katz's. My brother, three years older, told me about them many years later. I was five and six when we would drive from Long Island into Brooklyn and visit Stanley Katz's parents. As a teenager in Brooklyn, my mother had met Stanley, whom she wed in 1940 when she was twenty. In 1942, Stanley went to war. His platoon was captured by the Germans and held in a prisoner-of-war camp. After the war, most of the platoon returned to their families. But Stanley was given away, either by his name or by the *H* for *Hebrew* that the army stamped on the dog tags of Jews so that the appropriate chaplain would attend killed or wounded soldiers. Because Stanley was a Jew, the Nazis killed him, and my mother was a widow at twenty-three. In 1947, she married my father, and I followed in 1953, given bloodstained life through another's death, born of atrocity, beneficiary of Nazi hatred.

My generation, born during the post-war boom, did not greet the war's survivors nor mourn its victims; we did not recoil at the news of the camps nor rejoice in their liberation. To our parents' generation, the Holocaust was real and immediate: it was real to my mother, who lost her husband; and it was real to Naum Wortman, father of my childhood friend Marcel and survivor of Auschwitz, whose right arm bears the camp's scarred reminder, the inmate number the Nazis burned into it as a rancher brands cattle. But generations pass and scars fade, and even truth has been known to become legend. In a 1993 Roper poll, one-third of adults agreed it was possible that the Holocaust never happened. Twenty-eight percent of adults and 39 percent of high school students didn't know what the term *Holocaust* referred to; 50 percent of high school students couldn't identify Auschwitz as a concentration camp.

Since that poll, knowledge about the Holocaust has advanced little, while, according to one revisionist, revisionism "is springing up all over." The innocuously and deceptively named *Journal of Historical Review* continues to publish, in its words, "historical material from the Second World War onward, with an emphasis on revisionist viewpoints, especially of the 'Holocaust.'" The revisionists refuse to dignify even the very word; framed by quotation marks, it paints a fictional picture. A recent biography of Joseph Goebbels, Hitler's chief

> Revisionism has found its most congenial home where all rhetoric flows free: the Internet.

propagandist, argues that the Holocaust, to the extent it occurred at all, cannot be traced to Hitler. No written command exists ordering the extermination of the Jews; hence, there were no Hitler-inspired deaths.

Revisionism Flourishes

But revisionism has found its most congenial home where all rhetoric flows free: the Internet. A furor has erupted recently over the Worldwide Web page of Arthur Butz, a Northwestern University engineering professor. He uses his home page—part of Northwestern's Internet site—to broadcast his view that, as his 1976 book proclaims, the Holocaust is the "hoax of the twentieth century." Northwestern allows all of its faculty to place their home pages on the university's web server and has refused pleas that it deny access to Butz. Yet Butz is simply the most notorious of Holocaust deniers who have appeared on the web; revisionist home pages puncture the network like so many interwoven strands of barbed wire. One click takes you to a justification of Germany's imprisonment of the Jews in concentration camps; another to an exploration of the "myth" of the gas chambers; a third to an exposure of the "lie" that six million died. You can read biographies of leading Holocaust deniers, an attack on the Nuremberg trials as a miscarriage of justice, and a sympathetic review of a book suggesting that, with slight changes in strategy, Hitler could have won the war.

Related pages explore other aspects of what revisionists consider the Jewish menace: one click and you can read about Jewish terrorism in France or how the Jewish plan for world domination led to Jewish infiltration of the British royal family. No issue is unexplored; revisionist home pages, updated regularly, contain links to hundreds of articles, book reviews, and speeches. You can even scroll through a Holocaust calendar, chronicling significant dates when "proof" of revisionist history emerged.

Photo on previous page: Neo-Nazi revisionists routinely deny everything (including the body count) implied by the word "Holocaust." (Getty Images.)

To rebut the revisionists' claims, historians cite the testimony, physical evidence, and pictures documenting the Holocaust. And, indeed, the evidence is overwhelming. Yet the revisionists have answers—fantastical as they are—to all of it. Thus, charge begets response, and response begets rejoinder, until revisionist fantasies have entered the arena of historical debate. In the end, the revisionists are engaged on their own terms, as the questions for debate become not, "Was the Holocaust unique? What were the motivations of ordinary Germans?" but "Could the Allies really have constructed Auschwitz in three months after the war? Was the insecticide Zyklon B capable of killing human beings in gas chambers?"

> The revisionists rejoice in rebuttal, for point and counterpoint is the way of historical argument.

The Danger of Sound-bite History

No other historical event as recent and well documented—nor many far more distant and ethereal—is subject to a similar dispute. One might as well deny that World War II itself occurred or Vietnam or the last presidential election. The revisionists rejoice in rebuttal, for point and counterpoint is the way of historical argument. Yet this argument cannot be won. For if rationality could convince, convincing would be unnecessary and revisionism would not exist. Hatred and prejudice—the only basis for Holocaust denial—do not respond to reason. To engage in academic debate on the issue is to lend it a legitimacy it could never earn on its own.

Responses to revisionists reflect a natural desire to establish the truth of the Holocaust in the public arena. And perhaps the exposure of revisionist falsehoods is both necessary and inevitable. But even blinding exposure will open few eyes, for receptiveness to Holocaust denial does not stem from any nuances of the argument but from *the fact that the argument is made*. The Roper poll results reflect Americans' general ignorance of history and hence our receptiveness when a historical event about which most Americans know little is questioned. The poll did not reveal widespread doubt about the Holocaust; it revealed widespread susceptibility to suggestion. Polls routinely reveal that Americans know little about almost all major historical events and even have difficulty placing such events as the Civil War in the proper century. As a nation, we do not revere history; it does not surround us in every building and square as it does in Europe. By definition, it is old and therefore may be safely ignored.

Thus doubts about the Holocaust do not reflect considered opinion that the event may be mythical. Instead, just knowing—from the poll question, if from no other source—that the Holocaust is being questioned, many will respond that perhaps it didn't occur. If any other historical event were publicly and persistently questioned—and perhaps even if it were not—a comparable poll would yield similar results. Because we Americans are not grounded in the past, we are susceptible to sound-bite history; if it is suggested that an event did not occur, many are prepared to credit the suggestion. It is as if America has suffered a loss of collective memory. The Roper poll is a reflection of that loss. To paraphrase [Russian novelist Fyodor] Dostoyevsky, if memory does not exist, all things are possible.

> Because we Americans are not grounded in the past, we are susceptible to sound-bite history; if it is suggested that an event did not occur, many are prepared to credit the suggestion.

Teaching Subsequent Generations

Nevertheless, that the poll did not gauge particularized doubts about Jewish history is hardly cause for complacency, for, unique among indisputable historical events, it is the Holocaust that has been questioned. Debating the revisionists won't negate their claim to the popular imagination. If, indeed, the poll reflects more ignorance than doubt, then the debate must take place elsewhere. Our audience is not the revisionists but our children; our tool is not argument but exposition; our arena is not the journals but the classroom and the home. We Americans may ignore history, but we cannot escape it. For the past—memory—is all we ultimately possess, all that cannot be dispossessed, all we take with us, and all we leave behind. So we must preserve and renew memory lest it recede along with the past itself.

In an ethics class I taught recently, I devoted a section to the Holocaust. As I began, one student said jokingly but with at least a touch of uncertainty, "Oh, that didn't happen." (And now a subject of humor, how deeply the lie has entered popular culture.) I did not argue the point. Instead, I decided to let history judge. After an extended discussion, I showed my class films of the camps—to the limits of the students' tolerance, if not a touch beyond—the sunken eyes, walking skeletons, emaciated bodies bulldozed into mass graves. Afterward, no one joked, nor did anyone doubt. Discomfort is often the price of knowledge, for, if the Holocaust did not happen, we need not ask, "Why?"

Memory Preserved

In the summer of 1971, after graduating from high school, Marcel and I backpacked through Europe. We made a pilgrimage to Dachau in southern Germany, a death camp that had housed some 200,000 inmates. In 1965, the camp had been reopened as a memorial site. Two of the wooden barracks had been reconstructed. The camp, surrounded by a concrete wall with its brooding watchtowers, also housed two red brick crematoriums, which only two decades before had spewed black smoke and the stink of burning flesh over the German countryside.

The formerly barren barracks walls now bore pictures of Nazi doctors, scalpels aloft, cutting into Jewish brains in an elusive search for genetic deficiency—what was it, the Nazis wondered, that made the Jews inferior? We quietly toured the grounds and said little when we left, for the silent camp had told all.

In the fall of 1993, I visited the United States Holocaust Memorial Museum in Washington, D.C.: three floors of photographs, films, artifacts . . . and shoes—masses of shoes, piles of shoes like haystacks, shoes that once trod the dirt of Auschwitz, Treblinka, and Sobibor, shoes that would not be worn in the ovens or the graves and so survived the war. On the ground floor, in the bulging book of Holocaust survivors, I found the name Naum Wortman: Auschwitz survivor, Polish doctor, American husband and father.

> We must teach these stories in all their majesty and in all their sadness. If we pass on a reverence for the past, revisionism will die a silent death.

Visits to the Holocaust Museum so exceeded expectations that, after a year, it had to be closed for repairs, thus is memory preserved. As parents, teachers, and citizens we must ensure that, for each generation, memory is renewed. In an era of visual communication in which attention spans seem to shorten daily, changing Americans' attitudes toward their past will be no easy task. Yet the decline of the traditional text makes it even more urgent. Both Jewish and American history present majestic stories of triumph and survival: from the ashes of the Holocaust rose the phoenix of Israel. We must teach these stories in all their majesty and in all their sadness. If we pass on a reverence for the past, revisionism will die a silent death.

Sheldon Epstein, a part-time lecturer at Northwestern's engineering school, responded to Butz's web page by raising the issue in his engineering class. Outraged by Butz's views, Epstein acted when he discovered that his students knew little, if anything, about the Holocaust and assigned them a research project on it. He was later told by the university that his contract would not be renewed, in part because he had strayed from the course material. The Holocaust may not fit comfortably within an engineering curriculum, but it is relevant to much in the humanities and to much in our lives. We have many opportunities to pass on our stories.

My parents passed on their own histories. I do not recall when I discovered who Eichmann was or how I came to understand my mother's fevered cry. But somewhere between the ages of seven and eighteen I learned of the Holocaust; memory was handed down like well-worn clothes, a legacy embraced by each generation. My mother lived through the Holocaust and her husband was its victim. Soon the last survivors of that era will be gone. People perish, buildings fall, shoes tatter. But memory endures. So long as we preserve it, we too survive.

Allowing Holocaust Deniers to Defend Their Cases Exposes the Flaws in Their Positions

Deborah Lipstadt

Deborah Lipstadt is a professor of modern Jewish and Holocaust studies at Emory University and the author of *History on Trial: My Day in Court with David Irving*. That book is an account of the 1998 libel case brought against her publisher by British writer David Irving when Lipstadt accused him in writing of being a Holocaust denier. Lipstadt won the case, and the court ruled that Irving's manipulation of historical events—claiming, for example, that the Nazis created only concentration camps, not extermination camps—was tantamount to Holocaust denial. In the following viewpoint, Lipstadt states that she would not like to see Irving sentenced to prison for his radical beliefs. Instead, she argues that free speech laws should protect such

SOURCE. Deborah Lipstadt, "Attack the Lies, but Let the Liar Speak," *Times Higher Education Supplement 1730*, February 17, 2006, pp. 16. Reproduced by permission.

views, implying that only in the public forum listeners can recognize and, hopefully, discredit blatant falsifications of historical record.

The last time David Irving was in court, I was the defendant in a libel suit that he had brought against me for calling him a Holocaust denier, a racist and an anti-Semite. It was a case he lost on all accounts.

Next week [in February 2006], Irving will be back in court, this time on trial in Austria for violating a 1947 law against minimisation of Nazi-era crimes. The case revolves around speeches he gave in the country in 1987 in which he denied the Holocaust. He has been held in custody since last November, when he was arrested after returning to Austria to address a group of right-wing students. But despite the fact that Irving cost me tremendous time, energy and money defending myself, I hope the Austrian authorities release him.[1]

Fabricating History

In the libel trial, Irving was the cause of his own misfortune. While building my defence, we traced his sources and found that virtually every one of his claims about the Holocaust contained a fabrication, a distortion or a lie. This became dramatically clear in court. When asked by Richard Rampton, my barrister, how he could say that [Nazi airforce commander] Hermann Goering "goggled" at a certain exchange when there was absolutely no evidence that Goering was even at this meeting, Irving declared: "author's licence." On another occasion Irving, whose knowledge of German is impeccable, attributed to the pressure of preparing for the trial at 2 A.M. the previous day, a mistranslation that rendered the ominous field ovens—the incineration grids on which the Germans burnt their victims' bodies—into utterly benign

Despite having faced (and won) a Holocaust denier's libel suit, Deborah Lipstadt argues that revisionist views should be heard—and refuted. (**AFP/Getty Images.**)

David Irving: Hitler Was the Jews' "Biggest Friend"

There is a whole chain of evidence from 1938 right through to October 1943, possibly even later, indicating that [Nazi leader Adolf] Hitler was completely in the dark about anything that may have been going on. And I use these words very closely. I am sure you realize that I take a slightly different line from several people here. I would specify as follows: I would say I am satisfied in my own mind that in various locations Nazi criminals, acting probably without direct orders from above, did carry out liquidations of groups of people including Jews, gypsies, homosexuals, mentally incurable people and the rest. I am quite plain about that in my own mind. I can't prove it, I haven't gone into that, I haven't investigated that particular aspect of history, but from the documents I have seen, I've got the kind of gut feeling which suggests to me that that is probably accurate.

But when I was writing about Adolf Hitler, I had to look specifically about what he knew or didn't know. . . .

[The] evidence [I've uncovered] all goes to support my theory that probably the biggest friend the Jews had in the Third Reich, certainly when the war broke out, was Adolf Hitler. He was the one who was doing everything he could to prevent things nasty happening to them.

But he'd let the genie out of the bottle; he'd uncorked the bottle and the demon was there and he couldn't get the genie to go back in.

SOURCE. *David Irving, "On Contemporary History and Historiography." Remarks delivered at the International Revisionist Conference, September 1983.*

field kitchens. We pointed out that we had downloaded the same document with the same mistranslation from Irving's website two years earlier. He replied that he had made the same mistake twice.

Such things happened daily as Irving's claims to be a fastidious historian evaporated. When the judge declared him to be a "liar," a "falsifier of history," an "anti-Semite" and a "racist" whose conclusions were "unjustified," a "travesty" and "unreal," it was all over for him—certainly in serious historical circles.

Irving, his Austrian lawyer says, plans to plead guilty next week. But even this sounds a bit contrived. According to his lawyer, Irving has seen the light and now acknowledges the existence of gas chambers. His epiphany apparently came after he found fresh information in the Moscow archives in the 1990s. If this is the case, why was he still arguing that the gas chambers were fiction when he faced me in court in 2000?

> Laws against Holocaust denial contravene the notion of free speech. Although I am not a free-speech absolutist, I have never been comfortable with censorship.

Censorship Is Not the Answer to Holocaust Denial

But I would still like him to be released. As a result, some people have complimented me for my compassion and forgiveness. That is a lot of rot. I have no compassion for a man who has caused pain to Holocaust survivors and their families, and who seems to delight in spreading racism and anti-Semitism. If Irving were to admit his falsehoods and ask them—not me—for forgiveness, I might feel differently towards him. But he has shown no such inclination.

Rather than on grounds of compassion, I support Irving's release for ideological and strategic reasons. Laws against Holocaust denial contravene the notion of free speech. Although I am not a free-speech absolutist, I have never been comfortable with censorship. The recent [February 2006] debate about the publication of the Danish cartoons depicting Muhammad has given added meaning to that stance. If one outlaws Holocaust denial, one can outlaw such cartoons. If one outlaws such cartoons, one can outlaw what Shiites say about Sunnis, Orthodox Jews about Reform Jews, and Baptists about Catholics. Simply put: there is no end to the matter.

I recognise that Germany and Austria have a unique history that gives Holocaust denial a particular resonance. As uncomfortable as I am with such laws, I understand the impulse behind them in these countries. But I believe that they are not efficacious. Jailing Irving will render him a free-speech martyr and rescue him from his current state of oblivion. Let him return to the UK [United Kingdom] and be met by the thunderous sound of one hand clapping.

After all, this is a man about whom Judge [Charles] Gray [who presided over the Irving-Lipstadt case] wrote: "His falsification of the historical record was deliberate . . . (and) motivated by a desire to present events in a manner consistent with his own ideological beliefs even if that involved distortion and manipulation of historical evidence." Let him spend his time with those neo-Nazis and deniers still anxious to listen to him. They deserve each other.

Note

1. Irving lost the 2006 case and was jailed in Austria from February to December 2006.

Holocaust Denial in Muslim Countries Stems from a Desire to Enrage the West

Petr Pelikán

In the following viewpoint, Petr Pelikán claims that much of the Holocaust denial coming out of Muslim countries like Iran is not intended to convince the West that the extermination of the Jews did not take place. Instead, Pelikán asserts, the inflammatory rhetoric is meant to provoke Westerners by touching on a subject that is considered to be inviolable and above criticism. These Muslims, in the author's view, are trying to force Westerners to confront their hypocrisy regarding how the Holocaust and free speech intersect. Petr Pelikán is the non-professional head of the Consulate of the Republic of the Sudan in Prague, Czech Republic.

SOURCE. Petr Pelikán, "Holocaust Deniers and the West's Black Conscience," *The New Presence: The Prague Journal of Central European Affairs*, Winter 2010. Reproduced by permission.

Last summer [2009] I took part in a theological conference in Iran and witnessed a spontaneous debate between participants from several states. Actually, I noticed the man who began the debate on the first day of the conference. He was an Egyptian doctor from El Mansura. It was his first time abroad, and I had to explain to him how to use a hand lever shower at the hotel. In return he gave me a lecture on the firmness of faith and on the deception of Sunni Muslims. I was not surprised to see that he found a group of not-so-willing listeners and attempted to convince them that six million people could not have died in Nazi prison camps since there were not even that many Jews in Germany. According to him, those who left Europe to occupy Palestinian territories were also included in the death toll. The subject matter and tone of his argument was the same as spiteful Holocaust deniers who replicate under the fanatic regime of Iranian ayatollahs [religious leaders]. He did not receive the anticipated acknowledgement from his listeners, just unreceptive silence. So he also added that the extermination camps were just the invention of Zionistic propaganda; in his words, it would not be possible to round up so many people and keep them ignorant of their fate.

> Up until the day when the Iranian ideologists began to 'deny' the Holocaust, Islamic propagandists helplessly struggled to find and attack a sensitive spot for the West.

The first who reacted was a Dagestanian Russian: "Extermination camps did exist! Five men in my family died in extermination camps," was his icy answer to the Egyptian. "And after the war, eight more died. There is not a family in our town which did not lose one or more family members during the war. In the entire Soviet Union, more than twenty million people lost their lives." "Yes," said a young man with a Turkish name, "do not doubt the existence of the concentration camps or the incredible number of people who were killed there." From his strong accent and the German thoroughness of his subsequent lecture (which decidedly condemned the Nazi regime), I gathered that he belonged to the first or second generation of German immigrants. At the end he asked a surprising question related to both opinions: "If I was executed back then for not fitting in with the [Third] Reich's requirements, who would use me as a martyr today? The Germans, Turks, Muslims, or Shiites . . . ?"

Western vs. Islamic Invectives

Up until the day when the Iranian ideologists began to "deny" the Holocaust, Islamic propagandists helplessly struggled to find and attack a sensitive spot for the West. Western invectives, often true and often unintentional, touch on the innermost Muslim values to a far greater extent than the Western mind can possibly comprehend. On the other hand, Islamic invectives of a similar kind only meet amusement in the West, from which it affirms its European super-values and the basic postulates of freedom of thought and speech.

"How can someone kill just because of a caricature, even if it is a caricature of the prophet?" exclaims the West. "It is the same as if we were to offend Christianity," explains the East. "Well go ahead and do that, you have a right to do it," answers the West. "We can supply a plentitude of Jesus caricatures from our own stock if you would like. . . ."

"You breach women's rights," accuses the West! "We are protecting their integrity," replies the East. "You, on the other hand, have no decency; your women can behave like prosti-tutes and damage the family's honor." "If they want to damage it, they can damage it; they are free to decide

> They do not deny Nazi murders . . . but they do force the West to look in a mirror as they apply Western analytical practices and attitudes towards taboo topics.

Protests of Holocaust denials by Iranian president Mahmoud Ahmadinejad overlooked his propensity for remarks calculated to enrage Westeners. (**Associated Press.**)

what they want to do," answers the West again. "And you must allow them to do the same, because personal freedom is far more important than family honor."

An Untouchable Taboo

Muslims exclaimed with joy from all around the world when Iranians finally found an untouchable Western taboo, one which is even guarded by law in some countries. Certainly, Iranian propagandists are not primitive, and they are thoroughly prepared for an eventual debate with the aid of well-informed people with a European education such as that German Turk. They do not deny Nazi murders; they do not deny the persecution of the Jews, let alone endorse it; but they do force the West to look in a mirror as they apply Western analytical practices and attitudes towards taboo topics.

Iranians ask whether the concentration camp victims were first and foremost the inhabitants of the countries in which they lived, or were they Jews? Their propaganda does not argue about the numbers of dead, but they ask why does Europe ignore its extolled principle of civic nationalism on which its history is based and on the basis of which it criticizes the theocratic opinions of the Muslim faith? They direct your attention to historical and literary publications as well as works of art which depict Jewish suffering—monstrous and undeniable suffering—while emphasizing that theirs was not the only suffering created by the concentration camps. They wonder why Europe has placed topics related to this one particular group above the law, why one no longer has the right to freely express one's own—albeit perhaps false—opinion about this certain group? How is it possible that Europe has rejected—in only this one case—the honorable principle of "I don't agree with your opinion, but I will do everything I can so you can freely express it"?

Holocaust Caricatures in Teheran

A few years ago while I was in [Iran's capital] Teheran, I tried to see an international exhibition of Holocaust caricatures which was of course extensively covered by Western media. But in Iran, no one, including the media, cared about the exhibition; no one even knew about it. The government had obviously organized it as a gesture directed outside the country to convey that it knew how to provoke the West. While the exhibition was over by the time I found the exhibition hall, I have since had the chance to thoroughly study the catalogue. The pictures reminded me of the political caricatures of Jiří Žentel which were published by *Rudé Právo* (the official newspaper of Communist Czechoslovakia) in the 1970s (one featured Uncle Sam trying to shoot the dove of peace with cannons from an arms production factory). If the catalogue contained the same pictures as the exhibition, I can honestly claim that there was not a single drawing which aimed to ridicule or deny the tragedies and suffering which occurred before 1945. If someone sent those pictures to the competition, it only proves the integrity of the organizers who decided not to include them. As one might expect, most of the caricatures compared the Zionists' attitude towards the Palestinians to that of the Nazi regime—perhaps this crosses the ethical borders for some.

> Muslim "anti-Semitists" . . . is [a] very misleading and entirely European [term] since Semites are Jews as well as Arabs.

Two other large sections of the exhibition were directed at questions banned in the West: would the Israeli state have existed if Europe were not guilty of permitting the murder of their fellow Jewish citizens? Was that a legitimate reason enough?

The last section of the exhibition did not relate to the Holocaust in any way at all. It correctly anticipated the West's inadequate and uninformed reaction; it asked why the West could so easily mock the prophet when the exhibitions name alone was causing such a great outcry in Western media?

The Source of Propaganda

Let us now return back to the Egyptian doctor who could have easily competed with the most primitive skinheads and perhaps have even broken the law in some countries. Where did he receive his conspiratorial and false information about the Holocaust and other documents like the "The Protocols of the Elders of Zion"? Why has the Iranian propaganda apparatus distanced itself from these opinions? It is paradoxical that the rise of modern Muslim "anti-Semitists"—a term which is very misleading and entirely European since Semites are Jews as well as Arabs—has been partially assisted by world media and Western efforts to keep these taboos untouched.

Egypt, for example, views Iranian propaganda with the same abhorrence that the communist governments directed towards Radio Free Europe. Since the 1980s, the local regime has, not without reason, feared that Iranian influence could multiply and radicalize religious opposition (which the Egyptian government suppresses with the same brutal methods seen across the region). The country is therefore more exposed to news from global news agencies intended for Europe, though only after the content has been misinterpreted by several translations from several languages, mixed up with author commentaries, removed from the original context, and sometimes cut down to nothing more than a headline. The environment, which is awash with religious fanaticism and the frustration of repeatedly losing to Israel, will choose the meaning it wants to see, rather than the original meaning.

Could It Happen Again?

The young educated German with the Turkish name asked another question. He asked a question that even the militant anti-Israeli Muslim fanatics fear to ask, a question that even Europe does not want to think about. He said: "For me, Turkey is the country of my ancestors, a country we talk about at home, a country I have never visited, and a country where I certainly do not want to live. I am a German citizen with all the rights and duties that come with it, but I live in an environment which is inaccessible to 'real' Germans, and undoubtedly not all Germans consider me as one of their own. While I have studied in German schools, I also visit the local mosque and I have even visited a madrasah [Arabic educational institution]. My father has a German company, but it is only associated with other Turkish companies. When I marry, I will definitely marry a Turkish girl. That is how I was born, that is how I live, and I do not want to give up either one of my identities. But I also do not want to look for land somewhere in Anatolia where my family and I would have to flee because, I ask, how great is the difference between us and the pre-war Jews . . . ?"

Holocaust Reparations Threaten to Trivialize the Holocaust

Abraham H. Foxman

At the conclusion of the Holocaust, millions of Jews and other captives were liberated from concentration camps, forced labor, and hiding places. Since then, many companies, several banks, and the government of Germany have paid out restitution claims to the victims. Abraham H. Foxman worries, however, that the continued focus on reparations detracts from the quest to increase understanding of, and accountability for, the atrocities of the Holocaust. In the following viewpoint he argues that, while Holocaust survivors should be allowed to pursue claims against those who stole from or imprisoned them, the "industry" that has materialized around these claims threatens to rewrite the facts about why crimes were perpetrated against Jewish people in Europe and to refocus the discussion about the events from morals to money. Foxman is national director of the Anti-Defamation League, a preeminent Jewish civil rights

SOURCE. Abraham H. Foxman, "The Dangers of Holocaust Restitution," *Wall Street Journal*, December 4, 1998, pp. A18. Reproduced by permission of the Anti-Defamation League.

organization based in New York City. He was born in Poland and immigrated to the United States with his parents as a ten-year-old after surviving the Holocaust. He was saved by his nanny, who raised him as a Catholic during the war.

Now that Swiss banks have reached a settlement on Nazi gold, investigations into that country's Holocaust-era past are closed and the tide has turned to investigations of other countries, corporations, insurance companies and institutions like museums. This week [December 4, 1998] General Motors [GM] and Ford became the latest to be named for allegedly assisting [Nazi leader Adolf] Hitler's war effort. Also this week, representatives of 44 nations, Jewish groups and other interested parties gathered in Washington [D.C.] at the Holocaust Memorial Museum to examine a variety of issues related to Holocaust restitution, including insurance, property and stolen art.

Holocaust Activity Must Focus on Discovering the Truth

Certainly, individuals who had bank accounts, insurance policies or works of art that were stolen have a right to pursue their claims. But when these legitimate claims become the main focus of activity regarding the Holocaust, rather than the unique horror of six million Jews, including 1.5 million children, being murdered simply because they were Jewish, then something has gone wrong. A new "industry" has sprung up, spearheaded by lawyers and institutions, in an effort to get what they call "justice" for Holocaust victims. As a Holocaust survivor, I question for whom they speak and how they define "justice." The focus must remain on discovering the truth, on revealing and owning up to the past.

Lawyers have filed a civil suit against Ford, accusing it, through its German-based subsidiaries, of aiding the

Nazi effort, using slave labor and earning huge profits. Similar charges against GM are being documented in a book to be released next year. Both of the American

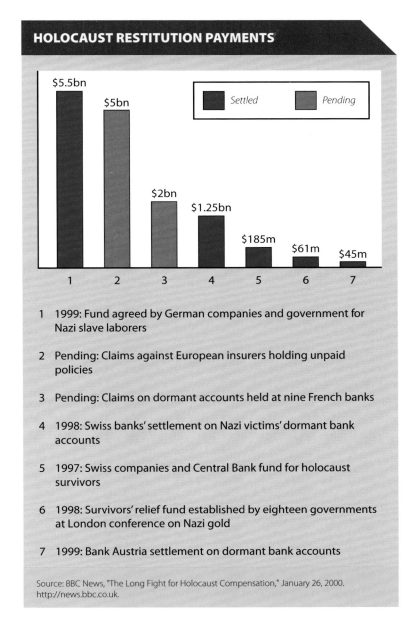

HOLOCAUST RESTITUTION PAYMENTS

Legend: Settled | Pending

$5.5bn
$5bn
$2bn
$1.25bn
$185m
$61m
$45m

1 2 3 4 5 6 7

1   1999: Fund agreed by German companies and government for Nazi slave laborers

2   Pending: Claims against European insurers holding unpaid policies

3   Pending: Claims on dormant accounts held at nine French banks

4   1998: Swiss banks' settlement on Nazi victims' dormant bank accounts

5   1997: Swiss companies and Central Bank fund for holocaust survivors

6   1998: Survivors' relief fund established by eighteen governments at London conference on Nazi gold

7   1999: Bank Austria settlement on dormant bank accounts

Source: BBC News, "The Long Fight for Holocaust Compensation," January 26, 2000.
http://news.bbc.co.uk.

Critics of lawyer Ed Fagan argue that his pursuit of compensation for various Holocaust victims was unseemly. (**Associated Press.**)

automotive giants had plants in Germany, established before the war, which flourished under the Nazi regime and continued operations even after the U.S. joined the war. What they "owe" for this in dollars and cents is not yet clear, but they do owe us the truth. While the corporations' current leaders cannot be held culpable for what transpired during the Nazi era, they will be judged by how they deal with it. They must vigorously, voluntarily and honestly confront that past by opening up their archives.

Seeking restitution is important, but at what price? Look at what happened in Switzerland [the banks paid out on accounts that had not seen activity since World War II but admitted no responsibility for colluding with the Nazis]. Yes, we got a check, but what about morality, reconciliation and confronting the past? The Swiss have yet to come to grips with the realities that their history, not the Jews, is their enemy, and that the settlement was not blackmail but a moral debt they should have paid voluntarily.

> A protracted discussion and debate [about Holocaust reparations] could bring a high price for the Jewish people, for history and for memory.

The Zealous Quest for Restitution

What concerns me today is the zealous quest for restitution without regard for consequences. A protracted discussion and debate could bring a high price for the Jewish people, for history and for memory. We need to understand that there is no absolute justice. Full justice could never be obtained from the Swiss, because we cannot put a price on the life of a child whom the Swiss turned back at the border when they saw "J" in his documents. We can only hope for a measure of justice, a symbolic justice that demonstrates an accounting and accountability.

Since the Swiss settlement there has been a rush for restitution. Some lawyers see it as an opportunity of a lifetime. Some politicians see it as a way to gain Jewish support. The $1.25 billion Swiss settlement would not have been achieved without the dogged efforts of lawyers and politicians, many of whom worked pro bono and because it was the right thing to do. But, I do not want Holocaust victims used as political footballs or tickets for financial gain. One of the lead attorneys in the Swiss case, Ed Fagan, is now traveling the world seeking new clients. In Poland he remarked that if Hitler moved across Europe from West to East looting and robbing, he, Mr. Fagan, would move from East to West reclaiming the losses. There is no place for ambulance chasers in this serious and sacred undertaking.

The disbursement of settlement funds has become a tug-of-war among vying groups and lawyers. I believe, first and foremost, that those who have claims should receive payment. Holocaust survivors without specific claims should be included in the disbursement of funds. After claims are satisfied and after needy survivors, who are mostly in Eastern Europe, are provided for, I suggest the remainder go to Israel. Not only would this make an important statement, but Israel has the greatest number of Holocaust survivors who need support. Israel has proportionately more children and grandchildren of survivors than any other nation.

Rewriting the Reason Why Jews Were Killed

I fear that all the talk about Holocaust-era assets is skewing the Holocaust, making the century's last word on the Holocaust that the Jews died not because they were Jews, but because they had bank accounts, gold, art and property. If you repeat it enough, you establish as "fact" that the reason the Jews were killed was because they had money. To me that is a desecration of the victims, a perversion of why the Nazis had a Final Solution [genocide], and too high a price to pay for a justice we can never achieve.

I was asked on a trip to Germany if I didn't think it was time to put an end to dealing with the Holocaust. I answered that there could be no end. We owe it to history and to the six million who died to teach the lessons of the Holocaust to new generations. Those lessons will be diminished and skewed by the efforts to put money over morality.

A New Form of Holocaust Commemoration Must Be Developed

Laura Duhan Kaplan

Since the end of the Holocaust, much writing and discussion of the event has focused on appropriate modes of commemoration to ensure that such an event never occurs again. In the viewpoint that follows, Canadian rabbi Laura Duhan Kaplan presents new ideas for commemoration ceremonies that cease to rely on the presence of Holocaust survivors who, after all, will not be around forever to lead such events. Kaplan describes these face-to-face commemorations, as well as the ways in which the Holocaust is currently commemorated in accordance with the traditional Jewish holiday Tisha B'av. She addresses the shortcomings of grouping Holocaust commemoration with this larger

SOURCE. Laura Duhan Kaplan, "A Future for Holocaust Commemoration," *Tikkun*, March-April 2007, pp. 49–53. Reproduced by permission from *Tikkun*: A Bimonthly Interfaith Critique of Politics, Culture & Society.

day of remembrance and suggests new ways of remembering and fostering understanding of the event. In creating a new mode of commemoration that breaks with current tradition, the author emphasizes the importance of experimenting with different means of communication and remembrance to ensure the continued passing on of history.

T he French-Lithuanian Jewish philosopher Emmanuel Levinas describes the core of ethical experience as one of confrontation: the face of one in need appears before us and calls us to respond. In his writing on the Holocaust, Levinas focuses on the ethical failure of perpetrators to recognize the face of the Other. In his essay "The Name of a Dog, or Natural Rights," Levinas tells of the failure of prisoner of war camp guards to recognize him and his fellow prisoners as human beings—something even a stray dog in the camp did not fail to do. In his lecture "Toward the Other," Levinas attributes this unforgivable moral failure to the late German philosopher Martin Heidegger.

Holocaust Remembrance Day rituals consist mainly of responses to a face. Typically, groups gather in the disturbing presence of one who suffered things they hope they will never even be able to imagine. They listen to a Holocaust survivor speak about his or her experiences. They watch the face of the speaker. The speaker's story of suffering moves the listeners to want to respond. Thus they respond with strong emotion rather than with pure intellectual analysis. They may even be awed that the speaker has the courage to remember, and find themselves pledging to honor the speaker by remembering as well.

This method of remembering the Holocaust cannot go on indefinitely. The generations that lived through World War II are beginning to perish. The method can continue, perhaps, for one more generation, as those who were raised by survivors re-tell the stories they

Photo on following page: The the Hall of Names at the Yad Vashem Holocaust Museum in Jerusalem. As time claims the last survivors of the Holocaust, new ways of addressing it should be developed. (Associated Press.)

heard from their elders and describe their own experiences as children of survivors. But, when this generation passes on, how will Holocaust Remembrance Day evoke a sense of connection to this historical event?

Commemoration and Communities

When I speak of commemoration, I have in mind remembering in a community, as a shared project. Commemorating does not require rehearsing historical events in excruciating detail, or the attempt to relive (or to cause others to relive) painful emotions. Instead, it is the practice of advancing certain values through symbolic reenactment of specific events. The aim of advancing these values is to create commitment to shared identities and communal projects.

> Commemorating does not require rehearsing historical events in excruciating detail, or the attempt to relive (or to cause others to relive) painful emotions.

In his book *The Ethics of Memory*, Israeli philosopher Avishai Margalit distinguishes between an ethical community and a moral community. An ethical community is given life by its ethos. Shared experiences, common memories, and bonds of feeling unite such a community. Families and close-knit ethnic enclaves are examples of ethical communities. The Jewish people—diverse as it is, and contested as its boundaries are—is an example of an ethical community.

A moral community shares mores. United by the fact of being human, members share an understanding of what constitutes decent behavior toward fellow human beings. They affirm a bare minimum of common values that make possible our co-existence on this planet. The entire human race is an example of a moral community.

The ethical community of the Jewish people and the moral community of humanity at large may have different reasons for remembering the series of events we now call the Holocaust. Many voices from the moral community of humanity have committed themselves to the project of standing guard against genocide. If groups cannot live without fear of genocide, then they cannot live in security. Without security, peace cannot exist.

Jews' Role in Moral and Ethical Communities

Jews are a part of the moral community of humanity uniting against genocide. In this role, we have engaged in various kinds of remembering: working with international bodies to identify and bring to trial those who led atrocities, writing histories that attempt to understand how a continent could bring itself to mobilize against genocide, and publicizing the deeds of those who resisted being drawn in to the genocidal machine.

As members of an ethical community, however, Jews have very different reasons for remembering the Holocaust. We remember it as a set of personal losses. Many of us can list as victims the family members we never knew, but watched our own relatives mourn for. Many of us can tell the war stories we heard from our parents, and some of us are the parents telling the stories. Any one of us can mourn the destruction of our great, diverse, vibrant, intellectual, artistic, political, European Jewish culture, as we contemplate the shrinking possibilities for diversity in contemporary Jewish life. In this mode, we remember the Holocaust because it has so deeply affected our way of being in the world, our sense of personal and collective identity as family members and as Jews. Although we can appreciate the very signifi-

> [Some] see the Holocaust as part of a repeating historical pattern of Jewish oppression and believe that the existing rituals of collective mourning are sufficient.

The US Holocaust Memorial Museum

Located only 400 yards from the Washington Monument, at the heart of the National Mall in Washington [D.C.], the United States Holocaust Memorial Museum (USHMM) is America's national institution for the documentation, study, and interpretation of Holocaust history. The world's largest and most comprehensive Holocaust museum, it also serves as the United States' memorial to the millions of people murdered during the Holocaust.

The museum, which came into being through a unanimous act of the United States Congress in 1980, is designed to be a permanent and powerful reminder to the American people and to the world that human-

kind must guard forever against the danger of another Holocaust. The museum is also an educational institution dedicated to teaching children and adults, through multimedia presentations, publications, and curriculum resources, and facilitating scholarship on the Holocaust through the Center for Advanced Holocaust Studies.

The USHMM's permanent exhibition, titled The Holocaust, tells the story of Nazi terror. While it focuses on the six million Jews who were murdered, the museum also tells the tragic story of gypsies, Poles, Soviet prisoners of war, homosexuals, the handicapped, Jehovah's Witnesses, and other victims of Nazi persecution. In addition, it rec-

cant acts of atonement performed by postwar Germany, these acts cannot erase our need as an ethical community for remembering this loss.

Including Holocaust Mourning in Existing Jewish Commemorations

Yom HaShoah (Holocaust Remembrance Day) is one part of a month-long [April-May] series of new holidays created since Israel's founding in 1948. Many liberal, secular, and Zionist Jews embrace Yom HaShoah with passion. They acknowledge the historical reality that the devastation of the European Jewish community led world leaders to recognize the State of Israel. They believe it is appropriate to mourn the losses involved in establishing ognizes the American liberators of the extermination camps and tells another story—about the failure of the free world, including the United States, to stop the Holocaust.

The building comprises 225,000 square feet of floor area on five levels above ground, and a below-ground concourse. The Hall of Witness serves as the museum's central gathering place, through which visitors pass to all parts of the building. This large, solemn hall, illuminated by natural light, resonates with symbolic references to the Holocaust. A deep crack, a symbol of the rupture of civilization during the Holocaust, runs down one wall of the hall.

The Hall of Remembrance, a hexagonally-shaped, skylit memorial projecting from the museum, is a spiritual space, designed as an area for contemplation and reflection as well as for public ceremonies. Along the hallway walls there are niches for candles—universal symbols of remembrance. The hexagon evokes the memory of the six million Jews murdered in the Holocaust.

SOURCE. *"Museums and Memorial Institutes,"* Learning About the Holocaust: A Student Guide. *Ed. Ronald M. Smelser. Vol 3. New York: Macmillan Reference, 2001.*

the State before celebrating its birth on Yore Ha'atzma'ut, Israel Independence Day, that same month. These Jews do not see the Holocaust as a node in a repeating pattern of Jewish suffering. For them, it is a unique historical event, part of a unique chain of historical events, and deserves its own special commemoration rituals.

Some Orthodox Jews, however, object to Yom HaShoah. Some of those who object are conservative and therefore do not accept the authority of modern innovators to create new holidays. Others are uncomfortable with the State of Israel instituting holidays because it was founded primarily by secular, rather than religious, Zionists. Others see the Holocaust as part of a repeating historical pattern of Jewish oppression and believe that the existing rituals of collective mourning are sufficient. In particular, they wish to mourn for the losses of the Holocaust on Tisha B'Av, the ninth day of the Jewish month of Av.

Tisha B'Av falls near the summer solstice, but unlike many other Jewish holidays, it is not spoken of as a seasonal holiday. The sense of mourning created on this day is given an entirely historical interpretation. The ninth of Av is the day on which the First Holy Temple, along with the rest of the city of Jerusalem, fell to the Babylonians in 586 BCE. Further, the ninth of Av is the day on which the Second Holy Temple, along with the rest of the city of Jerusalem, fell to the Romans in 70 CE. The ninth of Av is also the day on which the fortress of Betar fell to the Romans during the revolt of Bar Kochba in 135 CE, and it is the day that marks the expulsion of the Jews from Spain in 1492. We know from documents widely available that it is the day on which the Great Deportation of 350,000 Jews from the Warsaw Ghetto to Treblinka and other death camps began. And, depending upon the fate of the state of Israel, it may be remembered as the day before the evacuation of the Gaza Strip.

Creating a Mood for Remembrance

The rituals of Tisha B'Av include a twenty-five hour fast and small communal gatherings on the eve as well as the morning of the holiday. At these gatherings a mournful mood is set with low lighting, the use of special mournful tunes for familiar prayers, and the absence of refreshments or a communal meal. The biblical Book of Lamentations is read aloud. A carefully edited compilation of poetic laments from different authorial hands, Lamentations takes the reader through a winding maze of painful descriptions, political, cultural, and personal devastation; sadness; humiliation; guilt; a desperate will to survive; desire for revenge; hope; and profound questions about the role of God in a violent world.

Given the powerful themes of the Book of Lamentations, it is easy to see why many Jews feel that it speaks to a variety of historical tragedies beyond the one about which it was composed. Thus, the liturgy of Tisha B'Av has grown over the centuries to surround the reading of the Book of Lamentations with kinot—Hebrew for poetic laments and dirges—that mourn other historical losses. These include early medieval poems about the Roman conquest of Judea, as well as the murder of several Jewish communities at the hands of rioting mobs during the Crusades. In recent years, poems in memory of the six million lost in the Holocaust have been added—in sources that represent the poles of contemporary Judaism, including, at one end, prayer books produced by the Jewish Reconstructionist Federation, and, at the other end, prayer books produced by the Artscroll Mesorah (Tradition) Foundation. In a sense, these kinot are viewed as comments on, or extensions of, the content of the Book of Lamentations, and they help create the mood that helps the Book of Lamentations come alive with contemporary meaning year after year.

> "By defining the Holocaust as yet another attack on the Jews, the Holocaust is linked with an exclusively Jewish sense of being in the world."

Limiting the Possibilities of Holocaust Commemoration

Folding Holocaust commemoration into Tisha B'Av accomplishes several good aims. It keeps the meaning of Tisha B'Av current, and it makes use of a ritual structure that has evolved over centuries to create a moving ceremony. However, folding Holocaust commemoration into Tisha B'Av limits possibilities for understanding and remembering the Holocaust because the practice is based on a view of Jewish history as cyclical, rather than as one that can advance into new experiences and forms.

Such a view is not only pessimistic, but is based on an early medieval view of Jewish history that offers limited tools for understanding new historical situations.

Further, the practice of folding Holocaust commemoration into Tisha B'Av appropriates Holocaust remembering as a strictly ethical exercise. By defining the Holocaust as yet another attack on the Jews, the Holocaust is linked with an exclusively Jewish sense of being in the world, in which the Nazi genocide is part of a divinely ordained pattern of Jewish suffering. This is not compatible with the idealistic moral view that genocide ought to be both unthinkable and incomprehensible. And, consequently, it denies the fact that the Holocaust is an event of universal moral significance that affects humanity as a whole—not just the Jewish people.

Creating New Rituals and Literature

It might be possible to take what is most effective about Tisha B'Av and use it to create a Yom HaShoah commemoration for the future. Tisha B'Av could continue to be a holiday where we mourn a growing set of events that fit a particular pattern of Jewish history, and Yom HaShoah could continue to stand on its own. Yom HaShoah observances could include the rituals that build ethical ties, yet emphasize the universal themes that speak to a moral community.

A first step in doing so would be to create a central piece of literature. This could be a *Book of the Shoah* that takes the form of an edited compilation of excerpts from great Holocaust literature. The sources could come from a variety of writers coming from different positions: Jewish victim, non-Jewish victim, non-Jewish rescuer, Jewish or non-Jewish resistance fighter, repentant child of perpetrators, curious child of silent survivors, etc. The emotional topics could be diverse, ranging from brutality to helplessness, to heroism, to guilt, anger, sadness, and incomprehension. The finished *Book of the Shoah* would be short enough to read aloud in about half an hour. It would tell a coherent, yet multifaceted, emotional and historical story. It would confront listeners with voices from the Holocaust so that they would be moved to respond by a confrontation with a "face" in the Levinasian sense. If this project were undertaken right now, the result would likely not be the final form of the Book. Survivors and their offspring are still writing Holocaust memoirs, personal essays, novels, and poems. Even when such works are no longer being produced, it will take some time for a canon of the most compelling and most enduring works to emerge.

A second step might be to create appropriate group rituals surrounding the reading. They could be patterns of group movement, such as walking in a procession towards a goal or standing in concentric circles of unity; they could be songs sung in different languages by different composers. They could involve symbolic foods, such as the eating of a fruit that is mostly inedible and thus mostly wasted, followed by a resolution not to waste human life. Or, on a more hopeful note, something like an artichoke could be eaten, for which we remove the barbs to find the good at the center.

Experimentation Will Help with Remembrance

Such observances might turn out not to be popular over time. First of all, it would be difficult for the world moral community to sustain enthusiasm for an international commemoration once those personally involved and their offspring have passed away.

> Perhaps no single model [of commemoration] can work for all times and places.

Second, Jews might not support the lending of the ethical memory to the world moral community. We have long debated among ourselves whether we are in fact outsiders to an imagined world community, and whether we ought to consciously position ourselves as such. The Biblical prophets Isaiah and Micah, for example, hoped that the Jews' fall harvest holiday of Sukkot would be reinterpreted as an international holiday of peace and interfaith cooperation. In our time, [rabbi] Arthur Waskow is working to revive this hope by encouraging interfaith events during Sukkot (the Jewish harvest holiday). But the popularity of such practices is limited by the ambivalences Jews have about their status as world citizens.

Third, this model of a commemoration ceremony is based upon a certain cultural style of commemoration. It draws upon one particular Jewish conception of history, and upon one view of what constitutes a communal voice. Its elements—literature, poetry, and rituals involving light, food, and movement—are practices familiar to modern Jews. Perhaps, for a ceremony to have international appeal, it must draw on elements familiar to a variety of cultures. Perhaps no single model can work for all times and places. If so, the first goal would simply be to secure an agreement that commemoration is important for ethical and moral reasons.

Doubts notwithstanding, there is time and space for many experiments, and for many different conclusions. Clearly, now is the time to begin experimenting, so that we can remember—even after those who have carried the burden of constant face-to-face retelling are laid to rest.

CHAPTER 3

Personal Narratives

A German Jewish Man Remembers the Violence of Kristallnacht

Arno Hamburger

On November 9–10, 1938, German paramilitary forces and citizens across the country embarked on a campaign of destruction. Jewish homes and businesses were forcibly entered, ransacked, and robbed; Jewish men and women were brutalized, jailed, and killed. These events signaled the beginning of widespread violence against Jewish Europeans. In the account that follows, Arno Hamburger tells of his memories of Kristallnact (the "night of broken glass"), the name later given to this two-day period. Born and raised in Germany, Hamburger felt that Nuremberg was his home; however, with the rise of Hitler and the Nazis, he recalls feeling more and more like an outsider. Both his family members and friends lost their possessions and

SOURCE. Arno Hamburger, "The Night of the Pogrom of November 9–10, 1938 in Nuremberg," *The German Public and the Persecution of the Jews, 1933–1945*, Ed. Jörg Wollenberg, translated and edited by Rado Pribic (Amherst, NY: Humanity Books, 1996), pp. 11–14. English translation copyright © 1996 by Humanity Books. All rights reserved. Reproduced with permission of the publisher; www.prometheusbooks.com.

businesses during Kristallnact. He recounts the first reactions to these losses as well as the ongoing memories that stay with those who experienced these events.

It was cold on November 9, 1938. I was fifteen years old at that time. I was born in Nuremberg [Germany], like my father, but we were not allowed to feel at home in this city, which was always my hometown. Certainly I had a longer nose than my Aryan colleagues in school. As a joke someone called it "the key to the synagogue," and some people laughed themselves silly over this expression. I was a "Jewish pig," a subhuman. My family, the Hamburger family, had lived in Franconia [part of modern Bavaria in southeastern Germany] for four hundred years. My father was born in Schweinau.

> Before I rode to the store that morning of November 9, we knew that things would become worse and that it would be more than just a matter of someone calling us 'Jewish pigs.'

Tensions Rise on November 9, 1938

On November 9, 1938, I rode on my bicycle, as I did every day, to Erle, a Jewish electronics store in Johannis. I had been an apprentice there for a year, since I was not allowed to attend high school at Egidienberg. I was expelled from school when I beat up a fellow student who called me a "Jewish pig." Before I rode to the store that morning of November 9, we knew that things would become worse and that it would be more than just a matter of someone calling us "Jewish pigs." It was written clearly in the newspaper on November 9: "The German people are not taking this anymore." The reference concerned the assassination of [Ernst] vom Rath, the German diplomat, in Paris two days earlier by seventeen-year-old Herschel Grynszpan. The day passed by normally. In the evening at nine o'clock my father sent me to bed.

"Something will happen," he said. "We have to remain quiet." Shortly afterward there was a knock on the door. There were eight SA men [Nazi paramilitary soldiers]. "We have to search everything," they said. Nothing was broken, and none of us were touched. They searched the apartment and left. In my grandparents' house on Schweinauer Street the same thing happened—exactly the same thing: they searched and left again.

The Destruction Begins

My uncle Justin Hamburger lived on Landgraben Street. He was part owner of the Luma brush factory. I called him there, but he did not answer the phone. So my father sent me on my bicycle to his home. An SA sentry stood in front of the house and the lights were on inside. "Where are you going?" the SA man asked me. I said that I wanted to see my uncle. He responded, "You little Jewish pig, get going." Recently I had gotten used to this—the Jewish pig and the obedience. I returned home again, and on the way I saw that the SA had done a thorough job in the neighborhood. On Essenwein Street the synagogue was burning, Jewish stores were ransacked, the furniture was thrown onto the street, and the SA was watching so that no one would disturb the fire. The next day I rode again to the Jewish electronics store, Erle, in Johannis. It was no longer an electronics store—only a pile of broken furniture and equipment with a swastika on the wall. "It is the end," Mr. Erle said. "I do not have any work for you anymore." After this I returned to my uncle's apartment to find everything destroyed—glass was broken, books were torn apart, chairs and beds were cut into pieces, and the closets were broken into. Later, I read in the paper who had done these things on the night of November 9th. It

> Everything was broken into small pieces, and so, on the morning of November 10th, the victimized families had nothing left.

was not Mr. [Adolf] Hitler, nor Mr. [Julius] Streicher, and not the SA but supposedly a spontaneous uprising of the people.

Highly Coordinated Violence

On this night, hordes of SA men took their anger out, especially in the city of Nuremberg. First, they attacked the large stores, breaking the windows with the bars which they had brought with them, and then, they ransacked the stores with a mob which had already been informed that these events would take place. After this they proceeded to the dwellings where Jews lived. The non-Jewish tenants were instructed earlier to open the apartment house doors and, if the door was not opened, it would be broken down. Many of the "spontaneous" avengers were equipped with pistols and knives, while each group brought along axes, large hammers, and iron bars to force entry into Jewish homes. Several SS [Nazi troops] men had bags for collecting money, jewelry, paintings, and other valuables which they hauled off. The apartments were supposedly being searched for weapons because of a new law enacted the day before that forbade Jews to possess such items. Glass doors, mirrors, and pictures were broken. Paintings were cut with knives, and beds, shoes, and clothes were cut apart. Everything was broken into small pieces, and so, on the morning of November 10th, the victimized families had nothing left. Most had no coffee cups, no spoons, no knives, nothing at all. Any money that was found was confiscated along with valuable papers and savings books. The worst violence was aimed against Jewish apartment owners; both men and women were badly mistreated. The SA men drove a number of men to the jail. On the way there, the prisoners endured constant beatings and jeers from the crowd. The women who were also brought to the jail were usually released by the authorities after several hours. The men, among them boys under fourteen, were squeezed tightly into cells in great numbers. After more than a hundred males were turned-in in such a fashion, they were driven off in police trucks to the court jail and placed in its gymnasium. Toward the evening an additional number of Jews from the city of Fürth were brought in. The next morning around four o'clock all Jews under sixty years of age were deported to Dachau. The Gestapo officers arrested the secretary of the Jewish community, Bernhard Kolb. During the night SA men violently entered his apartment and struck him on the head. He was driven by car to the office of the Jewish Cultural Society, where he was imprisoned with other male prisoners. More and more Jews were brought in. Kolb reported that many Jews had been beaten severely.

Jews Pay for the Damage

On the night of November 9 to 10 nine people were killed in this violence in Nuremberg. On the same day the city coroner certified the suicides of ten Jewish citizens in Nuremberg. The Nazi lord mayor [Willy] Liebel reported to the city council that twenty-six Jews did not survive the night of the pogrom. That number was certified in the city registers; the number of Jews who died shortly after the so-called Kristallnacht [night of broken glass] is significantly higher. Since the cause of death was not indicated, however, it is difficult to say precisely how many of them were direct victims of that night.

Of the ninety-one murders which occurred during that night within the entire German Reich, nine were in Nuremberg. This shows the brutality with which the campaign was carried out in that city, even though the uncertified numbers which I have mentioned earlier are not included. During that night more than a hundred million marks worth of material damage resulted in Germany. At least 7,500 stores were destroyed; the damage to the glass windows alone surpassed six million marks. At least 267 synagogues were destroyed, and around thirty thousand Jews were arrested. They were sent to Buchenwald, Dachau, and Sachsenhausen concentration camps. The damage to the German economy was tremendous. However, the organizers of that night found a solution for this problem. On November 14, 1938, the Jews were ordered to pay a collective punitive fine of one billion Reichsmarks for the damages incurred to "the property of the people's community," as the perpetrators called it.

More Than Glass Was Broken

The last phase of the "solution to the Jewish question" had begun. That night was not only about broken glass and crystal; no, it was a night of murder in which more was broken:

> That night was not only about broken glass and crystal; no, it was a night of murder in which more was broken.

The dams of hate and prejudice were broken.

The concepts of friendship and humanity were broken.

Human hearts were broken; the confidence in a nation and in German people were broken.

No, it was not only a night of broken crystal.

A community broke here without recourse, a community of a nation. And everyone knew it and watched it, and no one could or wanted to help. One must have been deaf and blind during that night not to have known what was happening. If someone was able to say up until that point, "What business is that of mine?" or "I do not know anything," then everyone should have known after this night. It was one of the most shameful nights in German history. The last chance for a collective scream against further escalating injustice was lost. The crime which occurred in front of everyone's eyes was relegated to an everyday event because of the lack of action. This ordeal preprogrammed the beginning of the end of Jewish life in Germany and in Europe!

Memories of Kristallnacht Persist

I immigrated on August 22, 1939. Alone. To Palestine. On May 27, 1945, I returned to my hometown as a soldier in an English uniform. I stood at the Plärrer [a main square in downtown Nuremberg] and saw no houses, no streets, no trees, and almost no people. I had to think back to the night of November 9, 1938. I remembered the swastikas on the walls of the houses, the broken glass in the home of my uncle Justin, the ransacked stores, the burning synagogue, and the flames in the whole city. These memories will probably never die.

A German Woman Recalls Her Contact with Forced Laborers and Resisting the Nazis

Anna Rudolf

Anna Rudolf was a young German woman who came of age during the Holocaust. In the following interview, she recollects her contributions to the war effort as well as her personal opposition to Nazi treatment of forced laborers and Jews. As a young woman, Rudolf worked at a Nazi propaganda film agency in Berlin during World War II, cutting out shots of Adolf Hitler where he looked unfit for public appearance. During this time, she had firsthand contact with Russian forced laborers. Even though she felt that she should stand up for them and help them, her resistance to the Nazi leadership in her office was limited by the

---

SOURCE. Anna Rudolf, "Anna Rudolf: You, Good Girl!" *What We Knew: Terror, Mass Murder, and Everyday Life in Nazi Germany, An Oral History*. Edited by Eric A. Johnson and Karl-Heinz Reuband. Copyright © 2006 Eric A. Johnson, Karl-Heinz Reuband. Reproduced by permission of Basic Books, a member of the Perseus Books Group.

force with which her overseer opposed her interaction with the Russian laborers. Rudolf also recalls the kind gestures her family offered to those held captive in the work camp overseen by her father and the aid her father provided to a Jewish family he hid from the Nazis. Although she and her family provided assistance to those in need, Rudolf admits they were only somewhat aware of the maltreatment of Jews during the Holocaust.

I studied stenography with the goal of becoming a secretary and that is what I was. I was a secretary at the German State Library and I worked there for many years.

In 1937, when we came to Berlin, it was already in turmoil. Even at fourteen you are still aware of some things. At that time, you would hear things like, "Hitler deserves to have his head cut off," and "Who knows what is yet to come and what is going to happen? This place is seething!"

I had a friend whose father was a communist, an old communist and he would say, "Watch out, something's going to happen." And, when I was called up for service during the war, there were two colleagues of mine who were learning Russian, and I asked them why they needed to know Russian. Their answer to me was, "Watch out, they'll be here soon." So that's how it went.

During the war, every hand was needed and I was called up for service. I could choose between working at a cable factory or working as a uniform seamstress or working at a film duplication agency. Of course I chose the latter, but that turned out to be rather foolish. I ended up in the short film department and there I had to make copies of the films. I also copied feature films, but mostly I worked on film shorts. For example, if [Nazi leader Adolf] Hitler looked in bad shape in one of those film shorts, I would have to excise those strips. For this we had a closed box with a small slit in it and we had to throw away the strips so that nobody could somehow get hold of them.

Who determined what was to be cut out and what was to be kept?

The bosses certainly. Down below where the films were screened, we had a room for short films and also one for cinema films. After the films had been played, one then had to decide [which parts of the films were to be cut out], but the political filmstrips were always reviewed by the boss as well. Once this had been done, the films were then sent to the front. My job was to make copies of the films.

Contact with the Forced Laborers was Forbidden

All at once we got a number of Russian girls who had been brought to Germany [to work as forced laborers], and there were many nice ones among them. Our overseer was a guy who was walking around all the time in his SA [Nazi paramilitary organization] uniform making the rounds through all of the various departments. He would say to us that we were not allowed to talk with these women. "And why not?" I'd ask, "They are people just like us. They can't help it that they have to be here." So I often was at loggerheads with him. When I told my mother about this, she would always say, "Just you be careful or else he will have you taken away."

> Both my male and female coworkers were much more kindhearted, but they just looked away [from violence and mistreatment] and said nothing about it as they were all afraid.

Those girls were always hungry; they hardly would get anything to eat. Sometimes I would give one of them a slice of bread and butter, and they would say over and over again, "You, good girl! You, good girl!" There was one time that I was standing around talking with one of the girls who had the same first name as mine, Anna.

"What's your name?" "Anna." "I also Anna!" And, as we were talking like this, our overseer came by and saw that I was talking with her—he was always sneaking around like a cat—and he showed such a face. "What did I forbid you to do?" he said. And I said, "She's just as much of a human being as I am and as you are too." This made him mad and furious and he then sent me upstairs to the boss's office. But the boss actually was quite understanding. When I asked him why I shouldn't talk with these girls since we couldn't have any big conversations anyway as they couldn't understand much German and about all we could do was communicate through sign language, he understood me. "But take care," [he said]. "Watch out whenever that guy is nearby." Yes, indeed, he was a decent guy, a really decent guy.

Kindness Towards the Forced Laborers

Did you know where and how the Russians lived and how they were treated?

They all had plank beds to sleep on and they only got food to eat once a day. Nobody was allowed to speak to them. They had to work like dogs and they had to carry those heavy reels. And that overseer we had was a great big piece of crap. One time he even kicked one of the girls. Both my male and female coworkers were much more kindhearted, but they just looked away and said nothing about it as they were all afraid. Still, what I mean to say is that they were mostly generous to the girls, although you could easily notice that there were still some of them who hated those Russians.

> My father always acted humanely. He never pestered anyone or beat on him.

Because he could no longer hear properly, my father was put to work as a supervisor in a Russian work camp. This had a fence around it and there were about thirty men working there. They all lived in filth, really in filth, in the open air. My father later told me, "This is something I can't bear to look at anymore." My father then saw to it that they cut down some trees and had those thirty men make a roof for themselves. And he also got hold of some roofing paper so that it didn't rain on them. Despite this, they still froze and shivered. I can still remember how my mother and we two girls had gone over there twice, it was in Krampnitz, and how my mom couldn't bear to look at it all. And then she said, "Oh my word, how can we help these people?" So then what she did was gather up the cigarettes that she and my father got from the ration coupons and handed them [to the Russians] through the fence. They only just looked at her in amazement that they would get something from the Germans.

Then there was Christmas. This was to be the last Christmas before my father was taken to prison camp. Mom had baked cookies and she took a whole bucket full of them out there. At the time my father was a sergeant major and they treated him like an officer. And he had a young fifteen-year-old Russian boy who cleaned for him and shined and polished his boots. My father always acted humanely. He never pestered anyone or beat on him. And my mom gave the boy a big, beautiful plate full of cookies. Tears rolled down his face and we girls cried too. Then he stammered out to us, "Comrades too! Comrades too!" I've never seen anything like how they tackled those cookies. Despite everything, they shared with one another. And over and over again, they said, "You good woman. You good girl."

The Violence of 1938 and Fear of the Gestapo

What about persecution of the Jews? Did you, for example, experience the events of 1938?

That was really awful. When that happened I was walking down the street on the way to do some shopping and I thought to myself, "What is going on here?" We lived just around the corner from the synagogue near the Friedrichstrasse and so I could follow the whole thing. [In October] they brought all the Jews out of the synagogue and forced the men onto trucks. The women and children ran after them, screaming and yelling. Then they went away, and three days later the women and children were also picked up. I said, "Mom, what's going on?" And she said, "It's about the Jews. Who knows where they're going to?" [And then I replied to her], "But they are human beings just like us. Why are they being taken away? They haven't done anything wrong." Nevertheless, you had to keep your mouth shut.

And then [one day in November] when my mother and I were walking down the Neue Königsstrasse, it got really terrible. I had just wanted to buy myself a new pair of shoes, and then [we saw how] they were smashing in all of the shop windows and taping up Jewish stars everywhere and stealing like crazy. I could only stand there; I was devastated. Then my mom said to me, "Come on! Come on! Otherwise, we'll also be in trouble." It was awful. All the way down the street, one shop after another was destroyed, everything was smashed to pieces. They were in a rage, and what a rage, I tell you. One man continued to hit another man across the back with a truncheon. It was probably a Jew who could not get out [of a shop] fast enough or something like that. It was awful. Then I said, "Mom, I can't go on any farther. We have to go home, we have to turn back."

Earlier you said that there were all kinds of rumors going around in Berlin. Did you have a lot of fear of the Gestapo?

Well, yes, you knew people who even in the earlier days were wearing their party badges. And, since my mom often collected for the Winter Relief Organization, she knew a whole lot of people, and she would always tell us to be careful. And you knew yourself about how you had to be careful around this guy or that guy. It was always talked around about whom one had to watch out for.

We were always somewhat reserved and cautious because one basically had fear that one would be the next. And afterward, at the end of the war, it got really awful. Then there were soldiers hanging from the streetlights. They would have signs around their necks, saying "traitor" and nonsense like that. When some people were found trying to find a safe place for themselves, they would then be labeled as traitors.

> My parents had thought Dachau was a labor camp until it got around what kind of camp it really was.

Knowledge about the Concentration Camps Was Limited

Did you know before the end of the war about the concentration camps?

No. You would often hear things like, "He has been taken to a labor camp. He did something and he's been taken to a labor camp." But everything was covered up and kept concealed. Nobody knew anything specific. And then we'd hear again, "They packed that guy off to Dachau." My parents had thought that Dachau was a labor camp until it got around what kind of camp it really was. After that, everybody was afraid and nobody dared to say anything. . . .

Did you know from rumors before the end of the war about what had happened to the Jews?

Yes, even already during the war. That was all certainly talked about. But, as I was saying, it was always just said, "They are going to a labor camp." That they were gassed, and so forth, nobody had thought that. Nobody had thought that. Afterward, after the war, I worked with a Jewish woman whose father was a tailor. Her entire family had been taken away and her father had been forced to make and mend clothes in a concentration camp.

But her brothers and her sister and her mother were all gassed. She herself had been hidden and so both she and her father survived. Anyway, she told me all about what went on there, how they were beaten, and how they had to do all that work. That was certainly horrible.

My father had hidden a Jew. He was from our homeland [in Bavaria] and they had come here to Berlin. They had wanted to get out of here, and, by chance, they had run into my father on the Friedrichstrasse. At the time, my father had a brief leave from the military and so he ran into my father and my father hid him. My father never talked about where and how and what he did so that nobody could ever find out about this and so that we girls wouldn't blab or something.

A Polish Woman Recounts the Hardship of Life as a Teenager in a Forced Labor Camp

Lucyna B. Radlo

During the Holocaust, German troops invaded and subjugated many parts of Europe, forcing captives to work for the Nazi cause by producing a variety of wartime needs ranging from munitions to propaganda. In the following viewpoint, Lucyna B. Radlo recounts her experiences as a Polish girl in a Nazi forced labor camp. While not Jewish, she experienced extreme hardship working alongside her mother at a munitions plant in Germany, including meager food rations, insufficient accommodations, and mistreatment by the German overseers. Radlo admits that even though she believes the Jews have been

SOURCE. Lucyna B. Radlo, "9: Forced Labor Camp," *Between Two Evils: The World War II Memoir of a Girl in Occupied Warsaw and a Nazi Labor Camp*. Copyright © 2009 Lucyna B. Radlo by permission of McFarland & Company, Inc., Box 611, Jefferson NC 28640. www.mcfarlandpub.com.

justified in publicizing the suffering they experienced during the Holocaust, she wishes that more people were aware of the hardships experienced by other groups abused by the Nazis.

As we were leaving our beloved city [Warsaw, Poland] that was almost totally destroyed and burning, we continued to have the hope that one day soon we would be able to return, primarily to find our buried treasures, and to get our strength back and start our lives anew. Perhaps Mother's silent wish was eventually to marry Dr. Bruno Gutkiewicz and settle down. He lived in a lovely villa at that time in Gora Kalwaria on the outskirts of Warsaw. He had a steady, well-paying job as a chief doctor of veterinary medicine. (Little did Mother know that instead she was fated later on in her life to marry another vet instead, Dr. N. Proskuriakov.)

The freedom we seemed to have after leaving the combat zone of the city was short-lived. At the city limits, when we came to the surface, we were surrounded by German guards and marched several miles on foot to Pruszkow outside Warsaw to a streetcar depot. There we spent several days until we were transferred to a small facility, where we were housed in one of several barracks, all of which were filled to the brim. There was no food, water, or toilets. My acute intestinal problems continued, at times becoming worse. There was no way of getting any medication or to be seen by a doctor.

In Transit to the Labor Camp

Now in captivity, after a short stay in a heavily guarded transit camp, we went through a selection process in an open area. During this selection, a German soldier with a rifle told me to go to the left, Mother to the right, but Mother wouldn't let go of me. The infuriated soldier hit her on the head with his rifle butt, inflicting a fracture in her skull that she still had throughout her life. An officer, who was standing nearby supervising the selection process, intervened and let us both join the group on the right. Mother, bleeding from her head, and I, with the worst case of dysentery, together with many hundreds of fellow Warsaw insurgents, boarded a standing cattle-car train, 50 or so people to a car. This destitute flock filled the wagon like herrings in a barrel. It had one tiny window on the top and a bucket in the corner to serve as a toilet. No food, no water! And so, in the stuffy and smelly, closed and locked car, we were taken on a long journey to another transit camp in Erfurt (or Eisenach?) where German representatives, mostly *Lagerführers* (camp supervisors) came to select their future workers. Our future camp supervisor, Volkmann (whose first name or his rank, if he had one, I do not recall), happened to be a quite short man, dressed in a uniform and the typical knee-high leather boots. He carried a leather crop. His legs were quite bow-legged and as he walked he wobbled from side to side. One of his eyes was a glass one, replacing one he perhaps may have lost at the front.

> "The destitute flock filled the wagon like herrings in a barrel. It had one tiny window on the top and a bucket in the corner to serve as a toilet."

The Absence of Food and Physical Comfort in the Camp

Mother and I, together with five Jewish women and other Polish women, who had primarily come from the Prushkow camp, about 45 of us in all, were designated for a camp in Breitungen/Werra, Thuringen. It turned out to be *Lager Kirchberg*, the prisoners of which were forced to work at the *Metalwarenfabrik Scharfenberg & Teubert GmbH*, producing munitions for use on the various German fronts. Barbed wire enclosed the campgrounds that housed women, who were mostly Russians, Ukrainians, Poles and the five Jewish women I mentioned. A separate section, divided off by a fence, held men, who had come from France, Italy and Poland. The camp was guarded and was a short distance from the factory, in which local German citizens worked as supervisors or foremen. Armed guards accompanied each shift to and from the facilities of the plant. Apparently, because of the high percentage of foreigners working at the factory, the area escaped allied bombing, but supplies that were thrown down from allied planes and meant for the prisoners never reached us, most likely being retrieved by the local Germans. Upon arrival at the camp, we were photographed and we, physically, as well as our clothing, were disinfected. When the German guards, exclusively male, told us to strip, and Mother and I and the rest of us stood naked—I thought I would die of shame! While in a bath en masse we were watched by the guards. We were later issued identity documents (I asserted I was two years older to assure I would not be separated from Mother) and a ration card for food (reissued weekly and stamped each time we were fed), and assigned to one of the many long barracks. In ours, we met two Russian women. One was Vera, who came from Pinsk, and when we eventually became friends, it turned out that she knew Lyolya Ugrinowicz, who was Mother's cousin. In this designated barrack, we were assigned to a cot in a huge room. Since I was only a teenager and too young to be classified as "legally incarcerated," I wasn't assigned a cot of my own and therefore had to share one with Mother. The cots were two-decker type, as narrow as a stretcher. There were about 30 cots to a room. Each cot had a straw mattress, a straw-filled pillow, and a cover. Ours was the top bunk. The barracks were built very poorly, with walls made of thin boards, through which the wind and frost

> This watery *Kolrabi Suppe* [cabbage soup] was portioned out into metal bowls, together with bits of still clinging dirt and worms.

would blow in—there was always a draft of some kind! The roofs were full of holes through which, during the winter months, drops of melting snow fell. The monotonous noise of the drops brought us close to a nervous breakdown. One drop after another, endlessly. In the morning it wasn't unusual to see an icicle hanging over our heads and to find the cover and mattress damp. The walls would be covered with frost, and frost trees formed on the small, broken window panes, dripping and forming puddles on the bare floors. There was a small passage between the rows of cots, and in the middle of the room stood a potbelly stove, often cold due to the lack of wood for burning. The wind would blow the smoke back into the barracks through the long aluminum pipe that extended from the stove to the outside. The smoke was dense and inhaling it created headaches and breathing difficulties. After a while, Mother and I, together with the five Jewish women (the only Jewish women in the camp), were transferred to a small barracks, where there were three sets of cots—again, no cot for me!

Most of the inmates had only one change of clothing, since most of us were incarcerated during the heat of summer. It must have been the hottest August one could remember. All of us were not prepared for the cold days to come. Ironically, when fleeing Warsaw, Mother in the midst of the heat took her fur coat, for which many thought her mad, but in the camp during the bitter cold days and nights the coat was a lifesaver!

Days Filled with Work

A special track ran to the camp from the main railroad tracks, since the huge amounts of vegetables, mostly rutabagas and potatoes, were delivered by train. Dumped on the ground, they were hosed down to wash off clinging dirt, then chopped and cooked in a huge kettle. This watery *Kolrabi Suppe* [cabbage soup] was portioned out into metal bowls, together with bits of still clinging dirt and worms. A small piece of dark, stale bread accompanied the soup, and that constituted our daily meal. The severe rigors of wartime existence had left me weakened and emaciated, and coupled with prolonged severe bowel problems, I was constantly hungry. To help me recover my strength, Mother somehow was able to share with me her meager portion of daily ration. The German workers were allowed to bring box lunches or dinner pails and eat at designated tables, while those that were especially patriotic and didn't wish to waste time, ate at their machines. For us, regardless of which shift we worked on, there was no pause for lunch or dinner. How often we watched with envy the Germans eating their delicacies! Because of malnutrition, lack of sleep, and the harsh working conditions, it was an enormous effort to keep working until one's shift ended. The plant worked nonstop around the clock! We were allowed to go to an outhouse at a special hour only, not whenever nature's call came. The trip to the outhouse was guarded. During one of the trips to the latrine, we overheard two guards speculating as to whether the five women with us were not by chance Jewish? Once, later on, Mother and I were confronted by the *Lagerführer* with the same question. We both denied it, and from then on while we were in the camp the subject was not brought up again. One picture comes to mind about one of the trips to the outhouse. On this occasion, as usual, I stopped at Mother's station (her machine punched out bullets) when I found her standing but asleep, holding onto her coat, which was hanging on a hook. Her foreman, seeing her in this strange position, which perhaps may have lasted only a few seconds, dropped a heavy iron near her feet, scaring her almost out of her wits! In general, the noise of the several hundred heavy machines of various types was so loud that the foremen, in order to give commands to workers, had to shout at the top of their lungs. They liked to be mean and to make fun of us. Knowing that all of us were intimidated and scared for our lives, they took advantage of any given situation to spite us. The plant was a huge concrete building, poorly ventilated. Machines lined up one after another, leaving very little room for the operators or other equipment necessary for a given operation. Many critical machinery operations were manned by German foremen, sometimes German women. These were the trusted ones! We, the *Ost Arbeiter* (eastern workers) were not to be trusted and had to be watched. After all, what we were producing was ammunition that was used to defend their *Heimat* (homeland) and destroy ours! . . .

Acknowledging the Suffering of Poles

Ironically, the town of Breitungen/Werra, once a center for hundreds and hundreds of forced foreign laborers at *Lager Kirchber* engaged in the production of munitions and causing misery and suffering for so many, today, together with nearby Meiningen, is now listed as a *Christus Gemeinde* (a Christian community), and is said to be rich in arts and cultural traditions, with a very competent medical center. After the end of World War II we tried to find the Jewish women we shared the barracks with and whom we vouched for as Poles. We wrote to the contact addresses they gave us, but to no avail. Until this day we wonder if they were among the survivors when the camp was liberated in May of 1945. To this day, so many years later, whenever I say that my father died in Auschwitz and that Mother and I were captive in a labor camp, people are astonished and say with surprise: "I didn't know you were Jewish!"

> To me, as a victim and a survivor, it is very painful to see the Poles forgotten and not recognized for their horrendous sufferings.

The Jews have rightly done an excellent job of making the world conscious of their sufferings and of the persecution and enormous amount of atrocities inflicted upon them. The Nazis were intent on decimating the Jews of Europe. They were also planning the subjugation and destruction of the Slavs. Poland was devastated by the Nazi occupation. The subsequent Soviet domination resulted in delayed recognition of the enormous Polish losses. To me, as a victim and a survivor, it is very painful to see the Poles forgotten and not recognized for their horrendous sufferings.

A Holocaust Survivor Describes Auschwitz and His Survival

Thomas Buergenthal

The Auschwitz concentration camp in Poland is one of the most infamous of all the camps the Germans used during the Holocaust to exterminate Jews and others deemed unfit by the Nazis. More than one million individuals lost their lives at the camp in the gas chambers or as a result of starvation or of any of the other harsh conditions there. In the account that follows, Thomas Buergenthal describes his admittance to Auschwitz, the brutality of Jewish inmate guards against their fellow inmates, and the factors that allowed him to survive his time in the camp. Buergenthal reflects on his experiences, questioning man's inhumanity toward fellow humans and considers the resiliency of children in particularly difficult situations. Buergenthal was born in Czechoslovakia to German Jewish parents and immigrated in 1951 to the United States, where he eventually

SOURCE. Thomas Buergenthal, "Chapter 4: Auschwitz and Epilogue," *A Lucky Child: A Memoir of Surviving Auschwitz as a Young Boy.* Copyright © 2009 by Thomas Buergenthal. Reproduced by permission of Little, Brown and Company and Profile Books.

became a lawyer and judge focusing on international law and human rights.

I was ten years old on that sunny morning in the first days of August 1944 when our train approached the outskirts of Auschwitz concentration camp. Actually, as we were to find out later, we were on our way to Birkenau, located a few kilometres down the road from Auschwitz proper. It was in Birkenau that the gas chambers and crematoriums had been erected, and it was here that millions of human beings died. Auschwitz was merely the public front for the Birkenau extermination camp. Auschwitz was shown to visiting dignitaries, whereas Birkenau was the last place on earth many of the prisoners sent there were destined to see.

> Years later, when asked about Auschwitz and what it was like, I would reply that I was lucky to get into Auschwitz.

As the train moved closer and closer to Birkenau we could see hundreds of people in striped prison uniforms digging ditches, carrying bricks, pushing heavy carts or marching in formation in different directions. "*Menschen!*" ("Human beings!") I heard someone mutter, and I sensed a collective sigh of relief in our car. *After all, they do not kill everybody on arrival*, must have been the thought that flashed through everyone's mind. The mood in the car lightened somewhat and people began to talk again. "Maybe Auschwitz is not as bad as it has been made out to be," somebody said. I thought that it looked just like Henryków [a labor camp in Poland], only bigger, and that it would not be all that bad.

Making It into Auschwitz Alive

Years later, when asked about Auschwitz and what it was like, I would reply that I was lucky to get into Auschwitz. This response would invariably produce a shocked look on the face of the person who had asked the question. But I really meant what I said. Most people who arrived at the Birkenau rail platform had to undergo a so-called selection. Here the children, the elderly and the invalids were separated from the rest of the people in their transport and taken directly to the gas chambers. Our group was spared the selection process. The SS [Nazi troops] officers in charge must not have ordered it because they probably assumed, since our transport came from a labour camp, that children and others not able to work had already been eliminated. Had there been a selection, I would have been killed before ever making it into the camp. That is what I meant with my flippant remark about being lucky to get into Auschwitz.

Of course, when we arrived in Birkenau I did not know what to expect, nor that I had escaped the deadly selection process. As soon as we stepped out of our wagons on to the station platform, all men were ordered to line up on one side and women on the other. But for one brief moment a few months later, this was the last time I was to see my mother until we were reunited on 29 December 1946, almost two and a half years after our separation. We could not say goodbye properly because the SS guards were constantly yelling for us to move, hitting and kicking anyone who did not immediately do as they were ordered. I was too scared to cry or even to wave to her and stayed close to my father.

My father held on to me as we were marched away from the station towards a big building. Here we were ordered to take off our clothes and made to run through some showers and a disinfecting foot pool. Along the way our hair was shorn off and we were thrown the same blue-and-white striped prison uniforms we had seen from the train. It was at this point that my father whispered to me that we had made it, for only when we had received the uniforms could he be sure we were not being taken to the gas chambers.

From a Name to a Number

With that process behind us we were again ordered to line up and march. We must have walked for quite some time before we came upon rows and rows of barracks as far as the eye could see. Streets—actually unpaved roads—cut through the rows while high barbed-wire fences divided what looked like a large town into sizeable individual camps, each with its own gate and guard towers. Later I was to learn that these individual camps were identified by letters. Women were housed in camps B and C, men in camp D, and so on. Our destination was camp E, better known as the Gypsy camp. That camp had housed many thousands of Gypsy families. All of them—men, women and children—were murdered shortly before we arrived. Only the name remained to remind us of yet another horrendous crime committed in the name of the master race.

The entrance to the Gypsy camp, consisting of a movable barbed-wire gate, was guarded by the SS with their dogs. Once inside we were ordered to line up in single file behind a group of barracks and made to roll up our left sleeves. At one end of the line two inmates sat at a wooden table. Each of us had to move up to the table, state our name and stretch out our left arm. I was walking ahead of my father in the line, wondering what would happen next. Then I saw that the men at the table held what looked like pens with a thin needle, and that they were writing something on the outstretched arms after dunking the pens in an inkpot: we were being tattooed. When my turn came I was afraid that it would hurt, but it was done so quickly that I could hardly feel it. Now I had a new name: B-2930, and it was the only "name" that mattered here. The number, faded now, is still there on my left arm. It

> Now I had a new name: B-2930, and it was the only 'name' that mattered here.

remains a part of me and serves as a reminder, not so much of my past, but of the obligation I deem incumbent on me, as a witness and survivor of Auschwitz, to fight the ideologies of hate and of racial and religious superiority that have for centuries caused so much suffering to humankind. . . .

After we had been tattooed we were assigned barracks. Ours was a wooden structure like all the others in the Gypsy camp, with a mud floor that divided two long rows of wide, three-tier wooden bunks. Once inside we were greeted by a burly prisoner with a cane. This, I was to learn right away, was the *Blockältester* or barrack boss. He kept pointing to the bunks and yelling in Polish and Yiddish, "Ten men to each level!" Whoever did not move fast enough for him was hit or kicked. My father and I found a bunk, picked the middle level and were soon joined by eight other inmates. Then we were ordered to lie on our stomachs with our heads pointing towards the middle of the room. I can't recall whether we were given blankets, but I am sure that we had no mattresses.

Violence Committed by Jewish Kapos

Although we were not given anything to eat that evening, the very thought of food was forced from my mind by what happened later. Into the barrack strutted two or three well-fed inmates with canes and clubs. They wore armbands bearing the word *Kapo*. Kapos were inmates who, together with the barrack bosses, ran the camp for the SS and terrorised their fellow inmates day in, day out. Right after the kapos had greeted our barrack boss, one of them yelled in German, "Spiegel, you son of a bitch, get down. We want to talk to you!" As soon as Spiegel stood before them, the men surrounded him and started to hit him with their fists and clubs: on his face, his head, his legs, his arms. The more Spiegel begged for mercy and screamed, the more the kapos beat him. From what I could make out as the kapos yelled while beating him, Spiegel had apparently denounced one of them to the Gestapo [secret police] in Kielce [Poland], with the result that he had been sent to Auschwitz two years earlier.

Spiegel was soon on his knees and then flat on the ground, begging to be allowed to die. He was covered with blood and no longer really trying to protect himself against the blows that continued to rain down on him. The kapos then picked Spiegel up and began to push and pull him out of the barrack. We did not see what happened next, but we heard that the kapos had dragged him to the fence and that he died on it. Our camp, like the others in Birkenau, was enclosed by a high-voltage electric fence that emitted a perennial buzz. The fence separated those of us in the Gypsy camp from camp D on one side and camp F on the other. A single wire strung about a metre high and a metre from the fence on either side warned inmates not to get any closer lest they be electrocuted. Spiegel must have died after being thrown against the fence, or after crawling into it. Gradually, I came to realise that it was not uncommon for inmates to commit suicide by what was known as "walking into the fence."

> What is it in the human character that gives some individuals the moral strength not to sacrifice their decency and dignity . . . whereas others become murderously ruthless in the hope of ensuring their own survival?

Separating the Moral from the Ruthless

It is difficult not to wonder whether it ever occurred to these kapos that they were no different from Spiegel. He denounced fellow Jews to the Gestapo because he believed that he was thereby prolonging his own life, whereas the kapos allowed themselves to become the surrogates of the SS by beating their fellow inmates,

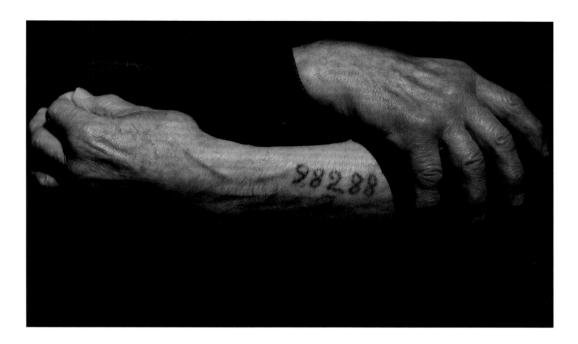

forcing them to work to total exhaustion and depriving them of their rations, knowing full well that such actions would hasten their deaths. And all that in order to improve the kapos' own chances of survival. Besides testing the morality of those who became neither informers nor kapos, the concentration camps were laboratories for the survival of the brutish. Both Spiegel and the kapo had been friends of my parents. Both had been with us in Katowice. At that time they had been my "uncles." I seem to recall that the kapo whom Spiegel had denounced had been a dental technician or dentist in his prior life; I never knew what Spiegel's profession had been. Had they not ended up in the camps, they probably would have remained decent human beings. What is it in the human character that gives some individuals the moral strength not to sacrifice their decency and dignity, regardless of the cost to themselves, whereas others become murderously ruthless in the hope of ensuring their own survival? . . .

Individuals sent to the Nazis' camps usually lost everything and gained a permanently etched serial number. (**Getty Images.**)

Luck Is a Combination of Factors

In the six decades since the end of the Second World War and my liberation, I have often wondered why or how I managed to survive the camps. These reflections are not brought on by feelings of remorse that I survived while so many others did not. Rather, my focus has been on the circumstances that allowed me to survive. If there is one word that captures the conclusion to which I always returned, it is luck. But luck is only the shorthand expression for a combination of factors that allowed me to make it. There was first the fact that during the ghetto and work-camp periods in Kielce I was with my mother and father, who not only cared for me but engrained in me the essentials of survival. Early on in Auschwitz, after I had already been separated from my mother, my father and I were still together. That allowed him to continue to protect me and to instruct me on ways to avoid ending up in the gas chamber. Of course, the fact that I was able to enter Auschwitz without being subjected to the deadly selection process on arrival was a major piece of luck. Had there been a selection, I would never have made it into the camp, and that would have been the end of my story.

> Luck is only the shorthand expression for a combination of factors that allowed me to make it.

A Child of the Camps

Once I was alone in Auschwitz, and later on in Sachsenhausen [another concentration camp], it helped that by then I was a little older and had become a true child of the camps in the sense that I had learned the tricks I needed to survive. I use the phrase "child of the camps" advisedly, because I have always felt that in many ways my survival instincts had much in common with similar traits I have observed in the street children of Latin America, who daily face many dangers and deprivations. These kids are frequently as young as I was, or even younger. I point to these children when friends express surprise on learning how young I was. Children, even relatively young children, learn to be cunning or street smart when circumstances demand, and they are fast learners when they have to be in order to live another day. When my own children were of the age I was during the war, I frequently wondered whether these pampered American kids or those of my friends could have survived in circumstances similar to mine. I am convinced that with some luck they could have, because the survival instinct in children is strong enough to allow them to adjust to the needs of their environment. Of course, what helped me was that I had a relatively long period of survival training. Who knows whether I would have lived had I arrived in Auschwitz from a normal middle-class environment and immediately had to face the brutal camp conditions. It was luck again that I had a gradual immersion into hell. (As I write these words I am not unaware how bizarre it is to use the word "luck" to describe such circumstances, but that is what it was, in its context.)

An American Soldier Experiences Hatred and Disgust at the End of the Holocaust

Stephen Shields

In May 1945, just before the conclusion of World War II in Europe, Stephen Shields was carrying out his duty as an army surveyor in Austria, chasing down the last of the fleeing German troops. In the account that follows, Shields recollects this period and the day he unknowingly came face-to-face with Nazi SS officer Adolf Eichmann, known as "the architect of the Holocaust." Shields describes the coldness in the freshly surrendered man's eyes and describes how their brief interactions forced him to remember the horror he experienced just one month prior in Nordhausen, Germany, when the concentration camp there was liberated. At that time, Shields saw the prisoners of the camp

SOURCE. Stephen Shields, "Triumph and Tragedy," *American Heritage*, 1989, pp. 82–91. Reproduced by permission of American Heritage Publishing.

as they marched lifelessly toward the town, looking for what he could only speculate—food, retribution, freedom. He also recalls the fiery hatred he felt toward the child soldiers of the Hitler Youth whom his battalion encountered on the way into town as well as toward the concentration camp guards corralled in the center of town.

It was the second of May, 1945, six days before the end of the war in Europe. We were members of Headquarters Battery, 608th Field Artillery Battalion, 71st Infantry Division—one of the spearheads of Ration's 3d Army, driving south through a conquered Germany toward Austria, the last unoccupied part of [Nazi leader Adolf] Hitler's [Third] Reich. Bridges over the Inn River, between Bavaria and Austria, had been wrecked by retreating German troops, but a large hydroelectric dam with a roadway on it was still intact, and that was our objective this beautiful spring morning.

There were four of us in the jeep. I was the driver, a twenty-one-year-old private first class. Beside me sat a first lieutenant, not much older than myself, and on the rear seat were a staff sergeant and a corporal, whose job was to operate the .50-caliber machine gun mounted between the seats. This was an unusually large weapon for a jeep at that time; some jeeps had .30-caliber machine guns, but most had none.

> The war was winding down rapidly. To our great relief the retreating enemy continued southward and eastward, across relatively open country.

This formidable weapon had probably been given to us because, as members of a survey section, we were often by ourselves, away from the rest of the battalion, plotting new positions for the howitzers [artillery] almost every day of that final, hectic offensive. Whatever the reason, we were glad to have it. . . .

A Suspicious German Prisoner

On the fourth of May we ran our last surveys. The gun batteries were placed in the positions we surveyed, but I don't think they ever fired from them. The war was winding down rapidly. To our great relief the retreating enemy continued southward and eastward, across relatively open country. There had been an ominous rumor that some German units might turn westward and make a final, suicidal stand in the Alpine Redoubt, a rugged area that would have been very costly to attack. But that didn't happen. Now they would be squeezed between the 7th and the 3d armies (our own 71st would be the most eastward division of all the Western armies when the war ended on May 8), the Russians moving west from Vienna, and the British 8th and American 5th armies coming northward from Italy. It was almost over.

The section came back glumly from the survey that morning to the hamlet in which we had spent the past day and a half, but not to the same attractive little house. Instead we went to the larger, rather drab house from which headquarters was operating. As we pulled up and stopped, we were mildly surprised to see a German soldier sitting on a low wall. A member of headquarters section explained that the man had just surrendered, and he was our prisoner until the MPs [military police] came for him. . . .

A Disconcerting Exchange with the Prisoner

Outside a light rain had begun falling. Our prisoner sat in a chair at one side of a desk, one arm resting on the desk, the sly, enigmatic smile still on his face. I noticed that his hands were clean, delicate, and manicured, like the hands of a woman.

We sat there in silence for a while, glancing at each other occasionally, and then, since this person spoke English, I asked if he thought the German army might

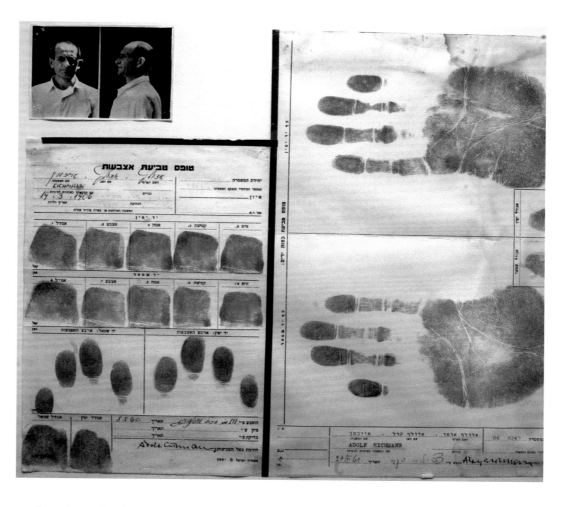

make a last-ditch stand somewhere. He said he was certain that wouldn't happen; the war would probably end in a few days. Dick [a fellow soldier] joined in, remarking on the scenic beauty of both Germany and Austria, an observation with which the prisoner naturally concurred. He then asked us what our ethnic backgrounds were, and when told both of us had British and German ancestors, he seemed pleased.

The conversation turned to the postwar period. I asked what he thought should happen after the war. He suggested that what he termed the Aryan countries—

Adolf Eichmann was apprehended in 1960 and convicted of war crimes committed during World War II. (Associated Press.)

Germany, Great Britain, the Scandinavian countries, the Netherlands, and the United States—form an alliance against the rest of the world, the non-Aryan world. Such an alliance could and should rule the world, he insisted. We thought this idea was preposterous and told him so. He was extremely displeased by our reaction, and the conversation died away.

After many minutes of silence he suddenly asked, "Are there any Jews in your company?"

My first impulse was to correct him and tell him that because we were artillery our basic unit was called a battery, not a company. My next reaction was a very uneasy feeling, one of dread. From the suddenness of the question, from something in his voice, and from the question itself, I got the strong impression that this man was obsessed with Jews. I decided to answer him civilly, to see where this topic might lead.

"Yes, there are a few—five or six, I think," I responded.

"Do you like them?" he asked sharply, almost accusingly.

"Yes, I like them!" I answered irritably. "Well, there's one I don't like very much, but it has nothing to do with his being Jewish. Why do you ask?"

There was a long pause, as if he were considering his answer very carefully. Finally he muttered, "Oh . . . no reason."

And that was the end of our conversation. It was as if he had suddenly realized it might be wise for him to stop.

Memories That Would Be Best Forgotten

Nevertheless, the brief exchange had made me recall something I didn't like to think about—the liberation by the division of the Nordhausen concentration camp. It had happened about a month earlier, in central Germany. Reconnaissance troops and infantry had come upon the place late one April afternoon, and we in the artillery learned of their discovery soon afterward. Nordhausen, a name unknown to most people, held about eighteen thousand prisoners, mostly Hungarian Jews. There were no gas chambers at Nordhausen; the people there were simply worked and starved to death. I learned later that the work they did was on the rocket weapons sent against England. When they died, their bodies were thrown into the ovens, which burned around the clock. The camp was populated by what appeared to be thousands of living skeletons.

The lieutenant got permission to go into the camp. He left most of the section in a farmhouse about half a mile away and went off with the sergeant and two of the corporals. I begged him to take me also, but he refused. I was angry as I watched them drive off without me.

So we had simply waited impatiently for our comrades to return. The owner of the house, whom we had permitted to remain, skulked about, doing his chores. He was extremely nervous and would not look at us directly. He knew what had been found half a mile away. There was an odd, sweet odor in and around that house that, though faint, was extremely offensive. It seemed to be unrelated to normal rural smells.

> [The corporal's] voice trembled with emotion as he told me of the camp. . . . I had trouble getting to sleep that night.

We realized later that the odor came from the ovens and chimneys of the camp, from the smoke of incinerated human bodies, and from a huge pile of rotting corpses in the nearby woods. That smell was, literally, the smell of death. And in that foul-smelling house there was a clammy, greasy film over everything that must also have come from the smoke.

The others came back around ten o'clock. They were very quiet and at first would say nothing about what they had seen. In the pale light of a kerosene lantern their faces were ashen, and we realized we were looking at men almost in a state of shock. After the others were asleep, one of the corporals began to talk to me. He was a person I regarded as a tough, hardened individual, but his voice trembled with emotion as he told me of the camp—of people so thin it seemed impossible that they could be alive; of the overwhelming stench, which almost made him faint; of recoiling in horror as a group of inmates tried to show gratitude for their liberation by touching him with skeletal hands that frightened him; of corpses still in bunks among the living, because no one had the strength to move them; of the ovens, still with bones and skulls in them; and finally of the monstrous pile of bodies in the woods. I had trouble getting to sleep that night.

An Army of Scarecrows

In the morning we started for the town of Nordhausen in convoy. This time we were near the end of the column. Somewhere between the camp and the town we came upon an incredible sight. Hundreds, perhaps thousands of the former inmates were walking toward the town in a great mass, through the fields on either side of the road. They were almost totally silent. The only sound they made was the rustling of their long, ragged coats against the grass of the fields. They looked like an army of scarecrows, a phalanx of living cadavers.

It was unclear why they had left the camp, where Army medical personnel were already beginning to help them. Perhaps they just wanted to breathe clean air again and walk in the open as free men. Perhaps they were simply after food in the town. Or perhaps they wanted to confront their tormentors and murderers. I never learned what happened when they reached the town. We gave them what food we could from our rations as we drove slowly through their ranks.

At one point along the road there was a dead horse, probably killed by artillery fire the day before. Two of its legs stuck rigidly into the air, and its entrails lay spilled on the dusty ground. Men were swarming over that dead horse like giant flies, ripping off pieces of flesh with their hands, and eating it. "My God! Look at that!" the sergeant exclaimed. "How hungry do you have to be to do that?"

"Mighty g—d— hungry!" muttered the corporal. Of the four of us, I suspected he was the only one who might have experienced hunger during the Depression.

Even In Defeat, Hitler Youth Incite Rage and Hate

A little farther along, our slow-moving convoy came to a complete halt. We had been stopped only a few minutes when we saw two boys approaching from the direction of the town, walking leisurely, defiantly along the other side of the road. They appeared to be about fifteen years old, and each wore the brown uniform of the Hitler Youth. They were blond, pink-cheeked, and healthy-looking. As they passed along our column, they were watched with silent hostility, contempt, or indifference. They paid little attention to us, except for an occasional arrogant glance in our direction.

When they were almost opposite my jeep, they suddenly saw the vanguard of the starving Jews, who were coming up behind us and were now walking on the highway. The two boys stopped in their tracks, utter amazement on their faces. Then, incredibly, they began to laugh. They nudged each other, pointed at the Jews, made comments, and continued to laugh uproariously.

It was as if the devil himself were hurling a final insult at those tormented people. We were dumbfounded and enraged. In desperation I turned to the lieutenant. "Sir! What should we do? Shoot them?"

"Are you crazy, Shields? That would be murder!"

"We ought to do *something*! They're the murderers! The whole g—d— country are murderers!"

Those two young Nazis probably never realized how close they came to dying on that road. I know others in that column were considering using their weapons to stop that laughter. I thought momentarily of shooting over their heads, to shut them up. Then I decided I would get out of the jeep, cross the road, and begin bashing in their faces with the butt of my carbine. But at that moment the convoy began moving again. The last I saw of this drama was the two boys and the army of living skeletons approaching each other. I have often wondered what happened when they met.

> On the faces of the people of Nordhausen I saw a single emotion, one I hadn't seen before in Germany: guilt.

Signs of Guilt in Nordhausen

Soon we were in the town, driving along the main street. It appeared to be one of the older, more picturesque towns, the kind one sees on postcards, with high-gabled, medieval-looking houses flanking the street. As in all the other towns we had entered that spring, white sheets hung from upstairs windows as a sign of surrender. But something was different in Nordhausen. The people here behaved differently. They saw the ugly mood of their conquerors, and they knew what had caused that mood. Instead of congregating along the main street, as was done in other towns, most remained indoors and watched our entrance silently and furtively from upstairs windows. In the other towns I had seen a variety of emotions on people's faces as we drove past them: fear, anger, hatred, anxiety, shock, dismay, and occasionally even friendliness. But on the faces of the people of Nordhausen I saw a single emotion, one I hadn't seen before in Germany: guilt.

There were pretty girls in those windows of Nordhausen. Blonde, shapely girls wearing colorful peasant outfits. A month earlier, when we first entered Germany from Alsace, we had regarded all Germans with hostility. Then, as the weeks passed, we had begun to relax a little, reacting to attractive members of the opposite sex in a more normal way. We would stare at them, smile at them, whistle at them, and occasionally make lewd remarks, in English and in German. But we did not smile at the girls of Nordhausen.

American Soldiers Lash Out at German Camp Guards

As we neared the center of town the unnatural silence was broken. Ahead of us we could hear angry voices, and we could see some sort of commotion. Uniformed men were milling about in a little parklike area up ahead on the right. As we got closer we could make out three kinds of uniforms—MP, infantry, and some unfamiliar green ones without insignia.

We were extremely puzzled. We had never encountered anything like this before. Then we began to distinguish the words being shouted. "Kill them! Kill them! Torture them! Beat them up! Give them to us. We'll take care of them!" As we got closer we could see that the MPs were halfheartedly trying to protect the men in green, while a group of infantrymen were striking at them with rifle butts and fists.

Suddenly I realized what was going on. "Sir! Those must be guards from the camp!"

In a moment we were abreast of the melee. The lieutenant and corporal remained stoically silent as we passed the ugly scene, but from the back seat the sergeant, his face contorted with rage, shook his fist and shouted, "Kill them! Kill the bastards! Kill the murdering sons of b—s!"

Something seemed to snap in my mind. I reached in front of the startled lieutenant and shook my fist.

> Something seemed to snap in my mind. . . . 'Kill them!' I cried. 'Kill them! Kill them! Kill them!'

"Kill them!" I cried. "Kill them! Kill them! Kill them!" A few minutes later we were again outside the town, in the quiet countryside, headed south. I knew I would remember the name of Nordhausen the rest of my life.

Face-to-Face with an Architect of the Holocaust

Having asked the questions that reminded me of these recent, grim events, our prisoner remained sunk in silence. After about an hour someone came up the stairs and said the MPs had arrived. Dick and I took the prisoner downstairs and out to the front of the house, where two MPs were waiting. They put him in their jeep and drove off. We said nothing to him, and he said nothing to us as he departed, but he gave us one final, chilling look with those cold eyes and that mysterious little smile. We both were relieved to see him go.

Exactly fifteen years later, in May 1960, I saw that face again and almost immediately recognized it, staring coldly from television screens and from the front pages of newspapers, beneath headlines saying EICHMANN CAPTURED!

The man I guarded for about an hour that day, and spoke with briefly, was surely Adolf Eichmann. Army records show that we were in the area in which Eichmann, according to sketchy biographical and autobiographical accounts, surrendered to American troops, on the day he said he surrendered. He said that he surrendered alone and in disguise, that disguise being a Luftwaffe corporal's uniform. In the last days of the war I saw thousands of surrendering Germans, but of those thousands I remembered only one face, and that one was identical to the face in the rare photographs of Adolf Eichmann. The ill-fitting Luftwaffe uniform had proved to be one of the great disguises of history and had earned for its wearer fifteen years of uneasy freedom, seventeen more years of life altogether. Fifteen years later that name and that face would be known by much of the world, but on that spring day in 1945, in that peaceful Austrian hamlet, there were only two who knew the terrible secret. There were only two who knew that behind that ordinary face with the icy smile there was unspeakable evil. There were only two who knew that the blood of innocent millions dripped from those manicured hands: Eichmann himself and his Creator.

CHRONOLOGY

1920 February 24: The German Workers' Party, started a year earlier, is reorganized as the National Socialist Democratic Workers' Party, also known as the Nazi Party. The party's foundational pillars include pan-Germanism, populism, racism, and anti-Semitism. Over the next decade, the party will establish a firm foothold in German politics through its propaganda efforts.

1921 A decorated German hero of World War I, Adolf Hitler, becomes leader of the Nazi Party.

1923 November 12: After a failed government coup attempt, Hitler is arrested and sentenced to spend one to five years in prison. He serves just over one year of the sentence but still finds time to dictate portions of Mein Kampf (My Struggle). The book is both an autobiography and a vehicle to solidify and publicize Hitler's ideas.

1930 September 14: The Nazi Party receives 18.3 percent of the Reichstag (German parliament) vote, earning 107 seats in the government. This represents a nearly ten-fold increase over the previous elections two years earlier.

1932 November 6: Public support for the Nazi Party roughly doubles from two years prior, with party members collectively receiving 33.1 percent of the vote and taking 196 seats in the Reichstag.

1933 January 30: Adolf Hitler is appointed chancellor of Germany by President Paul von Hindenburg.

February 27: The Reichstag building is burned down. Hitler uses the fire to institute a new constitutional clause revoking Germans' civil rights, such as freedom of speech, assembly, and press. Hitler invokes this clause to prosecute Nazi Party opponents and solidify his power.

March 22: A concentration camp is constructed outside of Dachau, Germany. Hitler's elite guard, the Schutzstaffel, or SS, uses the Dachau camp to hold political opponents.

March 23: Parliament approves the Enabling Act, enabling Hitler to establish a dictatorship in Germany and begin purging the "Jewish conspiracy" from German land.

April 1: The first of many nationwide boycotts of Jewish businesses, organized by the Nazi Party, commences. The boycott officially lasts only one day, but many local, small-scale boycotts continue.

April 7: With the passage of the Law for the Restoration of the Professional Civil Service, Jews and Nazi political opponents are denied the ability to serve in university or government positions. Over the course of the year, the Nazi Party enacts many similar laws depriving Jews and Roma (Gypsies) of German citizenship and forcing sterilization of Roma, the disabled, "social misfits," and blacks.

1934   June 30: During what is known as the "Night of Long Knives," Hitler's followers arrest and execute factions within the Nazi Party that do not agree with and support Hitler's policies.

August 2: President von Hindenburg dies. Hitler takes

227

the position of führer of Germany, leaving the presidency permanently vacant. With no constitutional limitations on his power, he is the absolute dictator of Germany.

1935   April 1: The Nazi government outlaws the Christian sect Jehovah's Witness following practitioners' defiance of Nazi laws requiring them to swear allegiance to the state.

June 28: With revisions to the criminal code, the Nazi government makes homosexuality a crime, and the Nazis begin persecuting homosexual men.

September 15: The Nazi government enacts the Nuremberg Laws, two measures that furthered Nazi anti-Semitic aims. The Reich Citizenship Law strips Jews of their German citizenship; later revisions revoke their right to vote or hold public office. The Law for the Protection of the German Blood and Honor disallows the marriage of Jews to German citizens; in addition, provisions in this law establish the definition of a Jew based on their lineage.

1936   August 1–16: The Nazi government succeeds at convincing the world that they are not persecuting Jews when Berlin hosts the Olympic Games. Many of the anti-Jewish boycott signs are taken down during the Games, and Jews receive a measured relief from the persecution they had been experiencing prior to the event. The Nazi government allows Jewish German athletes to participate in a few events.

1938   March 12–13: Germany marches into Austria and makes the country a party of the German Reich. This incorporation, known as the *Anschluss*, establishes Nazi anti-Semitic laws in Austria and leads to the widespread persecution of Jews.

June 14: A revision to the Nuremberg Citizenship Law requires Jews who own a business to register the company as Jewish. This allows the Nazi government to identify and deprive Jewish business owners of participation in the new German economy.

July 6–15: At the Evian Conference in France, the United States and many other nations refuse to modify immigration restrictions to allow more refugees from Nazi Germany to enter their countries.

August 17: The Nazi government passes a law, to take effect January 1, 1939, requiring all Jews who do not have typical Jewish names to adopt new middle names—"Israel" for men and "Sarah" for women—to identify themselves as Jewish. It becomes illegal for Jews to give their children "German" names as defined by a government list.

September 30: Great Britain, France, Italy, and Germany sign the Munich Pact, permitting Germany to incorporate areas along the Czechoslovakian border into the German Reich.

October 5: Responding to pressure from Switzerland, Germany begins to mark Jews' passports with a "J" so that they can be easily identified.

November 9–10: Following the assassination of Paris German embassy official Ernst vom Rath by Herschel Grynszpan, a Polish Jew whose family had been living in Germany but had been recently deported, the Nazis undertake the Kristallnacht—"night of broken glass"— pogrom. During the night, Nazis, with the help of Germans across the country, burn synagogues, loot and destroy Jewish homes and businesses, and attack Jewish men and women. Around 30 thousand Jewish men are arrested and taken to concentration camps, where they endure further violent treatment and are only allowed to leave on the condition that they promise to depart Germany. In all, nearly 100 Jews are murdered.

1939   March 14–15: Slovakia becomes a "protectorate" and puppet state of Germany shortly after declaring itself independent. The next day, German troops march into Bohemia and Moravia and establish a protectorate in the Czech lands as well.

May 13–June 17: The MS *St. Louis* ocean liner stops in both the United States and Cuba with more than nine hundred mostly Jewish refugees, but is denied entry in both countries. The ship is compelled to return to Europe.

August 23: Eastern Europe is divided with the signing of the Molotov-Ribbentrop Non-Aggression Pact by the Soviet Union and Germany.

September 1: World War II begins as Germany invades Poland. As a result of an Allied pact, two days later Britain and France declare war on Germany.

October: The Nazi government begins euthanizing mentally and physically disabled people defined as "incurable" and "unworthy of life." They are killed by lethal injection or in gas chambers.

November 12: Jews in German-annexed Poland are deported to areas in a region known as the General Government—areas in Poland not incorporated into Germany or the Soviet Union. The German government mandates that Jews in this region wear white badges with the blue Star of David.

1940   April 9–June 10: Denmark and Norway fall to German occupation.

April 30: Germany seals off the Jewish ghetto Lodz in Poland. It is the first major ghetto to be completely isolated and confines around 160,000 residents within its walls; they can leave only with permission from German authorities.

May 10: German invasion of the Netherlands, Belgium, Luxembourg, and France begins. In just over a month, Germany defeats the armies of each of these countries. In Southern France, Marshall Pétain creates the Vichy state which collaborates with the Nazi occupiers.

May 20: The first prisoners arrive at the Auschwitz I concentration camp in Poland.

November 15: The walls around the Warsaw ghetto are completed, sealing the ghetto and its more than 350,000 Jewish residents off from the rest of the world. Nearly 30 percent of the city's population is confined to an area measuring only 2.4 percent of the total area.

1941   April 6: German troops invade Yugoslavia and Greece.

June 22: German troops advance into the Soviet Union. *Einsatzgruppen*, mobile killing squads, follow, killing any Jews, Roma, and other "enemies" of the German state.

July 31: German air force commander and senior Nazi politician Hermann Göring enlists SS security chief Reinhard Heydrich to begin planning and initiating the "Final Solution" to the "Jewish problem"—the systematic mass murder of all the Jews in Europe.

September 3: SS guards at the Auschwitz concentration camp begin experimenting with Zyklon B gas to efficiently kill large numbers of "undesirables" in carefully prepared gas chambers. The initial experiments fail, and the prisoners do not die. After adjustments are made, the prisoners are led back into the gas chamber and eliminated.

November 26: The Auschwitz-Birkenau or Auschwitz II concentration camp is completed. It is the largest of all the camps and the most efficient of the death camps with its multiple gas chambers.

December 7: Japan bombs Pearl Harbor, drawing the United States into World War II.

1942   The mass killings of European Jews begin. German forces systematically transport Jews from all over Eastern and Western Europe to killing centers at the Auschwitz, Chelmno, Sobibor, Treblinka, and Belzec extermination camps. Over the course of the following three years, millions perish in the gas chambers at these camps.

1943   April 19–May 16: During the Warsaw Ghetto Uprising, Jewish fighters organize and defy German orders to transport ghetto residents to the extermination camps. It is the first major uprising in Nazi-occupied Europe.

August–October: Armed revolts ensue at the Treblinka and Sobibor killing centers.

1944   March 19: Hungary falls to German rule. Hungarian Jews are subsequently rounded up and sent to extermination camps.

June 6: British and US troops storm the beaches of

Normandy, France. The D-Day invasion coupled with the previous year's landings in Italy signal the beginning of the end of Nazi dominance in Europe.

June 22: Soviet forces advance from the east into German territory in Belorussia.

July: As Soviet forces continue their march westward, German forces transfer many of the prisoners in the concentration camps.

July 23: Soviet troops arrive at the Majdanek concentration camp in Lubin, Poland. German forces destroy the crematorium where bodies were burned, but they do not have time to destroy the gas chambers.

October 7: At Auschwitz, Jewish prisoners employed to remove corpses from the gas chambers stage a revolt. They blow up Crematorium IV, killing the Nazis guarding it. More than 450 prisoners are killed during the battle or afterwards as retaliation for the uprising.

1945   January 17: The "death marches" from Auschwitz west into the heart of the German Reich begin as Soviet troops advance towards the camp. Ten days later, Soviet troops liberate approximately 8,000 prisoners who were left at the camp.

April 11: US forces liberate more than 20,000 prisoners from Buchenwald, a concentration camp near Weimar, Germany.

April 29: US troops liberate around 32,000 inmates at Dachau.

April 30: As Allied forces approach Berlin, Adolf Hitler commits suicide in his bunker.

May: Almost 40,000 more prisoners are liberated from the Mauthausen and Gusen camps in Austria.

May 7–9: German forces surrender to British and US troops in the west (on May 7) and to Soviet forces in the east (on May 9). May 8 is dubbed Victory in Europe Day (V-E Day).

September 2: Japan surrenders after US planes drop atomic bombs on Hiroshima and Nagasaki, and World War II ends.

November 20: The Nuremberg Trials begin. An international military tribunal, consisting of judges from the United States, Great Britain, France, and the Soviet Union, tries twenty-one significant Nazi leaders for their crimes against humanity during the war. After nearly a year, eighteen of them are convicted—eleven are sentenced to death—for their roles in the mass murder of millions of Jews and other groups deemed unfit for life by the Nazis.

FOR FURTHER READING

Books

Yehuda Bauer, *The Holocaust in Historical Perspective*. Seattle: University of Washington Press, 1978.

Norman H. Baynes, ed. *Speeches of Adolf Hitler*. London: Oxford University Press, 1942.

Michael Berenbaum and Abraham J. Peck, eds. *The Holocaust and History: The Known, the Unknown, the Disputed, and the Reexamined*. Bloomington: Indiana University Press, 1998.

Jacob Boas, *We Are Witnesses*. New York: Henry Holt, 1995.

Tadeusz Borwoski, *This Way for the Gas, Ladies and Gentlemen*. New York: Penguin, 1976.

Michael Burleigh and Wolfgang Wippermann, *The Racial State: Germany, 1933–1945*. New York: Cambridge University Press, 1991.

Leonard Dinnerstein, *America and the Survivors of the Holocaust*. New York: Columbia University Press, 1982.

Alexander Donat, *Holocaust Kingdom: A Memoir*. New York: Holt, Rinehart, 1965.

Beret Engelmann, *In Hitler's Germany: Everyday Life in the Third Reich*. New York: Pantheon, 1986.

Helen Epstein, *Children of the Holocaust: Conversations with Sons and Daughters of Survivors*. New York: Putnam, 1979.

Norman G. Finkelstein, *Holocaust Industry: Reflections on the Exploitation of Jewish Suffering*. London: Verso, 2000.

Martin Gilbert, *The Holocaust: A History of the Jews of Europe During the Second World War*. New York: Henry Holt, 1985.

Daniel Jonah Goldhagen, *Hitler's Willing Executioners: Ordinary Germans and the Holocaust*. New York: Vintage, 1997.

Raul Hilberg, *Perpetrators, Victims, Bystanders: The Jewish Catastrophe, 1933–1945*. New York: Harper Collins, 1992.

Donald Kenrick and Gratton Puxon, *The Destiny of Europe's Gypsies*. New York: Basic, 1972.

Ernst Klee, Willi Dressen, and Volker Riess, eds. *The Good Old Days: The Holocaust as Seen by Its Perpetrators and Bystanders*. Old Saybrook, CT: Konecky & Konecky, 1996.

Lawrence L. Langer, *Holocaust Testimonies: The Ruins of Memory*. New Haven, CT: Yale University Press, 1991.

Primo Levi, *Survival in Auschwitz*. New York: Collier, 1973.

Richard C. Lukas, *The Forgotten Holocaust: The Poles under German Occupation, 1939–1944*. Lexington: University Press of Kentucky, 1986.

Vladka Meed, *On Both Sides of the Wall*. New York: Holocaust Publications, 1979.

Arthur Morse, *While Six Million Died: A Chronicle of American Empathy*. New York: Random House, 1967.

John Petropoulos and John K. Roth, eds. *Gray Zones: Ambiguity and Compromise in the Holocaust and Its Aftermath*. New York: Berghahn, 2006.

Anson Rabinbach and Jack Zipes, eds. *Germans and Jews Since the Holocaust: The Changing Situation in West Germany*. New York: Homes & Meier, 1986.

Alvin H. Rosenfeld and Irving Greenberg, eds. *Confronting the Holocaust: The Impact of Elie Wiesel*. Bloomington: Indiana University Press, 1978.

Sylvia Rothchild, ed. *Voices from the Holocaust*. New York: New American Library, 1981.

Aranka Siegal, *Upon the Head of a Goat: A Childhood in Hungary, 1939–44*. New York: Farrar, Straus & Giroux, 1981.

Avraham Tory, *Surviving the Holocaust: The Kovno Ghetto Diary*. Cambridge, MA: Harvard University Press, 1990.

Elie Wiesel, *Night*. New York: Bantam Books, 1986.

Susan Zuccotti, *Italians and the Holocaust: Persecution, Rescue, and Survival.* New York: Basic Books, 1987.

Periodicals

Mark M. Anderson, "The Child Victim as Witness to the Holocaust: An American Story?" *Jewish Social Studies*, Fall 2007.

Sue Andrews, "Remembering the Holocaust—Gender Matters," *Social Alternatives*, Second Quarter 2003.

Alon Confino, "A World Without Jews: Interpreting the Holocaust," *German History*, October 2009.

Elliot N. Dorff, "God and the Holocaust," *Judaism*, Winter 1977.

Stuart Eizenstat, "Holocaust Reparations," *Commentary*, January 2001.

Alan Farmer, "Hitler and the Holocaust," *History Review*, September 2007.

Eva Fogelman, "Rescuers of Jews during the Holocaust," *Tikkun*, March-April 1994.

Mark Grimsley, "(What If . . .) The Allies Had Bombed Auschwitz?" *World War II*, January-February 2010.

David P. Gushee, "Why They Helped the Jews," *Christianity Today*, October 24, 1994.

Daniel Gutwein, "The Privatization of the Holocaust: Memory, Historiography, and Politics," *Israel Studies*, Spring 2009.

Erwin Knoll, "The Uses of the Holocaust," *Progressive*, July 1993.

Berel Lang, "Six Questions on (or About) Holocaust Denial," *History & Theory*, May 2010.

Meyer Levin, "They Saved the Children," *Saturday Evening Post*, January 20, 1945.

David Lindquist, "The Coverage of the Holocaust in High School History Textbooks," *Social Education*, October 2009.

T.S. Matthews, "The Meaning of the Eichmann Trial," *Saturday Evening Post*, June 10, 1961.

George Michael, "Deciphering Ahmadinejad's Holocaust Revisionism," *Middle East Quarterly*, Summer 2007.

Roger Moorhouse, "Beyond Belief," *History Today*, September 2010.

Bruce W. Nelan, "The Goods of Evil," *Time*, October 28, 1996.

Jan M. Piskorski, "From Munich Through Wannsee to Auschwitz: The Road to the Holocaust," *Journal of the Historical Society*, June 2007.

Graham Smith, "The Geography of the Holocaust," *Geographical*, September 1994.

Leon Wieseltier, "After Memory," *New Republic*, May 3, 1993.

Ruth R. Wisse, "How Not to Remember & How Not to Forget," *Commentary*, January 2008.

Websites

British Library's Voices of the Holocaust (www.bl.uk/learning/histcitizen/voices/holocaust.html). This specific site maintained by the British Library houses primary source collections (in written and audio formats) of witnesses to the Holocaust.

The Harvard Law School Library Nuremberg Trials Project (http://nuremberg.law.harvard.edu). The Harvard Library maintains more than 1 million pages of documents and testimony taken from the trial of accused Nazi war criminals during the postwar, international Nuremberg Trials and subsequent U.S. Nuremberg Military Tribunal.

The Holocaust History Project (www.holocaust-history.org). This website, put together by academics, legal professionals, and amateur historians, provides a range of contributor essays on various aspects of the Holocaust, including the Nazi agenda that led to the exclusion, deportation, and eventual murder of millions of European "undesirables." The site also maintains a question-and-answer page on Holocaust denial and revisionism.

The Nizkor Project (www.nizkor.com). The Nizkor Project collects links to Holocaust-related documents, photographs, and websites and catalogs them under topic headings. The site provides some material from Holocaust deniers in order to show the faults of these pernicious views.

Remember.org (http://remember.org). Remember.org (A Cybrary of the Holocaust) is a repository of survivor stories, photographs, and research material on the Holocaust. The purpose of the site is to provide education to and to share Holocaust culture with visitors.

The United States Holocaust Memorial Museum Online (www.ushmm.org). The website showcases events at the museum, but also offers avenues for students and teachers of all education levels to learn about the Holocaust.

INDEX